D1232834

The Susquehanna River Guide

Christopher Beatty

Ecopress

Corvallis, Oregon

Ecopress

"Books and art that enhance environmental awareness"
1029 NE Kirsten Place, Corvallis, Oregon 97330
Tel: 1-800-326-9272
Email: ecopress@peak.org
WWW: www.ecopressbooks.com

Copyright 1998 Christopher Beatty

Photo Credits and Acknowledgments:
Greg Mentzer: Smallmouth bass, back cover middle and bottom.
Barry and Cathy Beck: Front cover, back cover upper.
A special thanks to river guides Tim Holschlag, Greg Mentzer, and Brian Schumaker for editing and assistance. Aerial photography courtesy of Ed Guthrie. Flies and lures photographed by John Ledges. Illustration and design by Chris Beatty.
Printed in the U.S.A. on 100% recycled paper (20% post-consumer) with soy-based ink.

Library of Congress Cataloging-in-Publication Data
Beatty, Christopher
        The Susquehanna River Guide / Christopher Beatty
            p.   cm.
        ISBN:0-9639705-6-9
        1. Susquehanna River—Guidebooks. I. Title
    F157.S8B42   1998
    917.4804'43—dc21   98-29619

10 9 8 7 6 5 4 3 2 1

Table of Contents

Part I. Enjoying the Susquehanna

Part II. River Corridor Maps

A Susquehanna Smallmouth

Dedicated to my father, Robert Eugene Beatty, who introduced me to my first river – Michigan's AuSable.

Feeling truant
I bagged the last cluster and
headed for a nearby bramble
With the companionship of a splash of single malt
all to ponder:
What god have I?

'Tis the defiant Douglas streaking silently skyward
While the chainsaw watches;
'tis the crimson blush of steel fish
and those perfect fins
fanning over clear cobble;
'tis the sound of falling water
and the whisper of the mist that feeds it;
'tis the bloody grass and the lowly bug upon it
More for the rough-skinned that eats him;
'tis the jag that draws me up
and the scornful eye and talon
Of the raptor that bests me
despite my summit;
'tis all this and more

It's the way they play
Together

Chapter One

The Physical River

The Susquehanna is the largest and longest river flowing to the eastern coast of the United States. The river drains roughly 28,000 square miles in Pennsylvania, New York, and Maryland. It is said that the Susquehanna is the longest non-navigable river in North America at 444 miles. Although the river is about a mile wide in the lower reaches, many shallow sections of ledgerock make passage difficult for all but small craft with minimal draft.

This guide highlights many of the recreational opportunities on the river from the Chesapeake Bay up the main stream to just above Wilkes-Barre, Pennsylvania. The lower West Branch of the Susquehanna from Williamsport downstream is also included.

The huge volume of water from the Susquehanna causes the entire north end of the Chesapeake Bay to be primarily fresh as opposed to salty. Fifty percent of the bay's fresh water comes from the Susquehanna. Typical flows are 20,000 to 50,000 cubic feet per second(cfs), but can be over 200,000 cfs during normal spring floods. During these times the river can rise more than fifteen vertical feet at the gauge at Harrisburg relative to typical summer lows.

1

The figure below shows the flow for the 1996 water year (10/1/95—9/30/96) as well as the 20 year average for the period from 1976 to 1996. During 1996, an exceptional flood of over 500,000 cubic feet per second occurred. The flood is off the scale of the graph since it dwarfs the data for most of the year. Although this was a major event, it was only about half of the flow that occurred in 1972 during the landfall of hurricane Agnes. Often referred to as the "Johnstown flood" because of the devastation near Johnstown, Pennsylvania, the flood killed many people and produced the largest flows ever recorded in many rivers.

Susquehanna Flow at Harrisburg

.... 20 Yr. Ave. '76-'96 ⎯ 1996

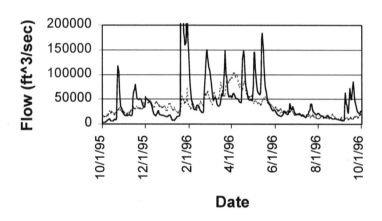

Peak flow rates for each of the past fifty years are shown on the following page. A tremendous amount of variation is possible year to year and day to day. This is important to remember when you are considering heading out for a day on the river for floating or fishing. The best approach is to call ahead and see what level the river is running. The National Weather Service maintains a recording of the river height and flow at 814-234-9861 which is updated daily. At press time, another toll-free line was being maintained by Pacific Power and Light for the Safe Harbor area. The number is 1-800-692-6328 and reports not only the flow at Holtwood, but some other useful information such as temperature, clarity, and reservoir regulation levels. Alternatively, if you are a web surfer, you can check out the following URL:

http://wwwpah2o.er.usgs.gov/rt/rt_table.html

When the page loads, click on the Susquehanna and select the station nearest the area you plan to visit. The numbers discussed below reference the Harrisburg gauge, but you may want to learn what to expect at another gauge near your destination. While you are out surfing, you may also want to check out the Environmental

Susquehanna Annual Peak Flow at Harrisburg

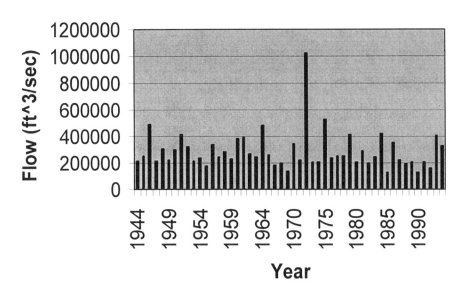

Protection Agency's "Surf Your Watershed" page. Start off with the following URL:

http://www.epa.gov/surf

If you're like most of us, the number of days you can get away is limited, so use them wisely. If the stage or height of the river is above 6 feet at Harrisburg, stay home and cut the grass. The fishing will probably be poor, and the boating and wading can be dangerous.

Hiking and birding can still be good if the ground is not too muddy from recent rain.

A stage of four to six feet is still high and typically muddy water, but can still be worthwhile in quieter areas. Wading is still a challenge if you can't see the bottom and fishing may be limited to large or noisy flies and lures. Many fly-fishermen will still not bother.

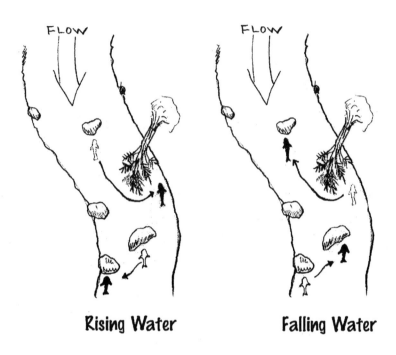

Rising Water   ## Falling Water

Water levels of three to four feet represent normal low water and will usually have good visibility for fishing and boating. If the river rises appreciably, it also tends to be swift and muddy. During the rise, fish respond by either hunkering down behind mid-stream cover or moving to protected areas near the banks, sloughs, and eddies. Here the current is slower which requires less energy and also allows some of the heavier silt to settle out. When the river starts to fall, the fish move back toward the center to avoid being trapped in a pocket or side channel which is shallow or dry at lower stages. It is unfortunate that some fish, especially fry, do get caught in these areas and are left high and dry. This is particularly a problem if the level change is very rapid as can happen with some hydroelectric facilities. For fishermen, the key to remember is that a rise in river level may push fish to areas near the bank. The diagrams on the previous page illustrate this idea.

Wading is a great way to explore the river during low water. For the warmer months, felt-soled wading shoes or cleats are all you need since the summer water temperature is typically 70-80 °F. I have waded in the Susquehanna downstream of the Brunner Island power plant when the warm discharge area was over 100 °F. This temperature is more like a hot tub than a river and is too warm for nearly all gamefish because the water cannot hold enough oxygen for survival. It's best to move away from the discharge at these times. In the Fall and Winter months, however, these discharges are like fish magnets. Water temperatures in the discharge zone of 50 to 60°F are common during this time and quite welcome for both fish and fishermen.

When using temperature to judge fish activity, remember that the actual number is not the only important factor. Another important aspect to consider is the trend of the temperature over the last few hours. If the present temperature is relatively near optimum but moving away from the best value, the fish will be less active than if the current temperature is good and moving toward the peak value. On some days, a few degrees of warming can trigger fish into feeding. Carrying a thermometer will help you detect these trends. The exact value of the optimum temperature for a given species of fish also varies, so use the numbers listed in the following chapter as a guideline.

Chapter Two

A Fishing Primer for the Susquehanna

The Susquehanna is a dynamic and productive fishery despite more than a century of abuse from coal mining, poor farming practices, inadequate sewage treatment, and a host of other sins. Hopefully, the worst is behind us as pollution control legislation passed twenty to thirty years ago has helped improve water quality since then. Further protection could make this river even better. Even in its current status, the Susquehanna is one of the best smallmouth streams in the eastern United States. Smallmouth bass sizes have increased since 1991 because of the enactment of a special 15 inch minimum size limit. These progressive regulations (from the Fabridam in Sunbury to Holtwood Dam) have already improved the fishing and should help to insure quality fishing for the future.

Gamefish of the Susquehanna

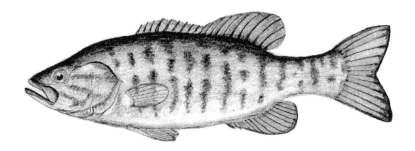

Smallmouth Bass

For many Susquehanna fishermen, the smallmouth is the premier gamefish. This fish is strong, voracious, and plentiful — everything you look for in sportfishing. Oddly enough, the smallmouth is not native to the watershed, but was imported from the Ohio River basin in the 1800s. Since then, it has flourished and established itself throughout the river. Typical fish in the river run between eight and fourteen inches, with occasional bruisers up past twenty inches. The smallmouth packs a lot of fight per pound, so be ready.

Finding smallmouths in the river is not difficult (consistently finding the larger specimens is another story). These predators prefer a small sheltered space near active water. This is sometimes referred to as "fishing the seams". The narrow zones between fast-moving water and quieter pools or pockets are seams. These zones or spaces may be either horizontal or vertical in nature. I'll explain what I mean by that. Horizontal shelter includes mid-river islands, weed beds, and other lateral structures which create holding areas for fish. As the diagram shows, the cushion on the front side of the obstruction will often hold fish, as will the pocket at the tail of islands or weed beds.

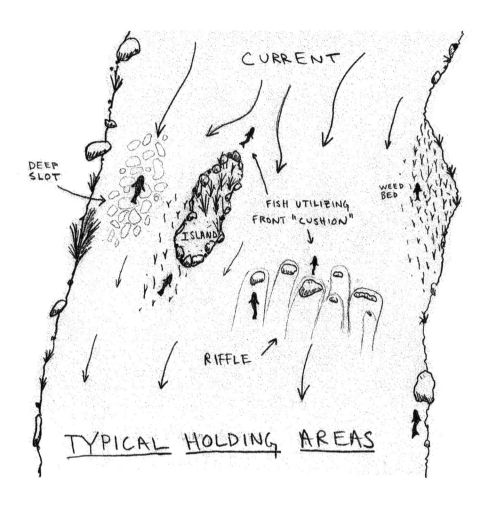

CURRENT

DEEP SLOT

FISH UTILIZING FRONT "CUSHION"

ISLAND

WEED BED

RIFFLE

TYPICAL HOLDING AREAS

River riffles are also an important type of cover for many game fish. Similar to the island, there is a cushion or quiet zone just upstream from the head of the riffle. Many fish wait here for the incoming "chow." There may be many fish in the riffle itself, but if it is too shallow or lacks large boulders, they may be rather small. Behind the riffle, larger fish wait for crayfish, hellgrammites and fry to be washed out of their holding areas between the rocks. These food items give an indication of the sort of imitations that should be used.

Vertical Structure created by ledgerock

If the riffle is deep enough, it can create vertical structure. Vertical structure is created by the bottom structure's relationship to the total water column. The carved out structure of the river bottom has many areas where ledges of rock are formed. These ledges create pockets for the fish to hide in and wait for food to drift by. If the bottom is covered with boulders or various sizes of rock, good cover will also be present. Certain types of fishing are more difficult in this water, however. Sinking lures and flies are more likely to get hung up on a rock or ledge bottom. There are times when this is just part of the game, but floating or shallow-diving attractors will often be successful without the frustration. In the deepest channels (more than 8-10 feet), there is a boundary layer of quiet water near the bottom even with relatively little additional structure. Fish will sometimes be found in these areas, especially in very bright light conditions. Smallmouth will also be found near overhanging bank structure, particularly if the river is rising (see physical river section).

Smallmouth bass prefer clear or slightly colored water and indirect light. Actual water clarity conditions can range from totally muddy to crystal clear. Both ends of the spectrum can be challenging. Water with near-zero visibility will probably mean poor fishing success. Under these conditions, the fish can't see the bait and it's not clear that they feed much then anyway. When the visibility rises to a foot or more, fishing often improves. At this time, use larger, noisier lures and flies to get the fish's attention. Bright colors and larger offerings are in order. If the clarity improves so that you can see more than four feet into the water, you will probably want to scale down both the size and color intensity of your lure. Very clear water also means that it is extra important to move quietly and cast past the optimum fishing zone to avoid spooking fish with a big splash. A finer leader may also be necessary. Sometimes the water clarity is not consistent throughout the river and predators such as smallmouth will use this to their advantage. There are times when a tributary stream is either clearer or muddier than the main river. Fish will use the seam between the clear and muddy water to hunt small fish. The murkier water provides cover and concealment, but allows access to the clear stream where bait fish may be spotted. Foam or froth lines create a similar effect. Look for this type of seam near the downstream side of dams.

Light is another important variable for smallmouth. Look for cover that provides shade, especially during sunny days. Morning and evening are often the best fishing of the day because the fish feel safer hunting in the limited light. In lieu of shade, added water depth reduces light intensity and provides greater security from most predators except larger fish.

Remember that season and sunlight also control water temperature. Smallmouth will feed over a wide range of temperature, but get progressively more active as the water warms in the Spring and take surface imitations more readily when the water temperature rises above the mid-fifties.

The Springtime also includes the spawning period, typically in May when the water temperature rises above about 60 °F. Right before the spawn, smallmouth are often quite aggressive, but remember to return all fish caught during this time so that they can reproduce. This is particularly important for smallmouth since they are not particularly prolific egg layers, averaging a couple thousand eggs per nest. Studies on some waters show that predation of eggs by other fish can occur within minutes of pulling the parent fish away from the nest. However, even with this loss, current research generally indicates that other factors such as water temperature and food supply are the limiters to juvenile fish reaching maturity.

During the actual spawning period, one or more female smallmouth deposit eggs in the nest and then depart. The eggs hatch in two to four days. Although the adult male will defend the nest, the young fish leave the nest after approximately a week. Bass grow quickly and reach sexual maturity to repeat the cycle, typically in three years. At this time, they are approximately ten inches long. Trophy fish of eighteen to twenty inches require eight to ten growing seasons, so remember to release at least most of what you catch. The nest is usually one to three feet in diameter in a few feet of water. After spawning, the fish typically are a bit inactive for a couple weeks. After recovering, the fish resume feeding. Warmer temperatures during the summer months spread smaller fish throughout the river. Larger fish venture into shallower areas early and late in the day to forage. Surface activity is often excellent during these periods.

As Fall approaches, the water temperature will drop, but fishing can be excellent as the fish feed heavily to carry them through the winter. Water temperature is near optimum throughout the river and fish often feed all day. Depending on which expert you believe, either the pre-spawn or the fall feeding binge is the best time of year to catch really large smallmouth bass.

As Winter sets in, fish become less active, but can still be caught by fishing near the bottom of deeper channels lined with large rocks or other cover. Another alternative is to fish the warm water discharges from power plants. Fish not only remain active, but are drawn to these areas in the winter.

Smallmouth will readily attack plugs or flies that look like crayfish (rust, brown, olive), minnows (chartreuse, white, silver) and hellgrammites (brown, black). Spin-fishermen can also use spinners while fly fishermen experience exciting sport using surface poppers, white fly imitations, minnow imitations, and nymphs. The photographs show a selection of appropriate imitations for both the fly-fisherman and the spin-fisherman.

The only two fish you are likely to confuse with a smallmouth are a rock bass or a largemouth. Rock bass are easy to distinguish because of their multiple rows of horizontal spots. Largemouth bass live up to their name. Their jaw hinge extends past the back of the eye while the smallmouth's does not. Color is more variable, but smallmouth tend to be bronze to olive with barring on the gill cover and vague vertical barring. Largemouths tend to be greener and have a more horizontal orientation to their marking. The jaw line is the best way to tell.

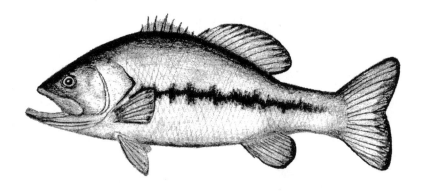

Largemouth Bass

While not as common, there are plenty of the smallmouth's larger cousin in the river. They prefer the lake-like habitat behind each of the dams, but are found scattered in adjacent portions of the river as well. The largemouth will find a quiet area with cover and often wait for food to swim by. They will eat many of the same things as a smallmouth, but his diet leans toward larger food, especially fish. Spin-fishermen can put plastic worms, spinner baits, and surface plugs all to good use. Fly-fishermen can use large surface poppers or streamers. Leech patterns also arouse this fish's interest. The largemouth prefers warmer water (68°F-88°F) than the smallie, so summertime is the best season for this fish. The largemouth is also more tolerant to varying degrees of turbidity, salinity, and bottom structure than the smallmouth.

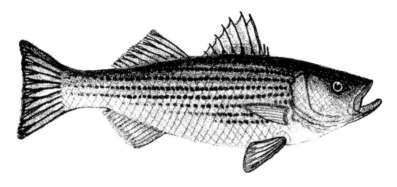

Striped Bass and Hybrids

Striped bass and striped bass/white bass hybrids called "wipers" are found in Lake Conowingo and downstream from the dam to the bay. The striped bass represents one of the few pieces of happy news in terms of fisheries management. The population of stripers was seriously depleted in the 1970s due to over fishing and habitat loss. Very restrictive regulations have allowed this fish to recover enough to be a valuable sport fishery once again. Hopefully, we can learn the lesson present in this history.

Stripers come up into the Susquehanna flats and lower river to spawn in late March or early April. Striped bass seek out the fresh/salt interface in the estuary and spawn just above this area. In the Susquehanna, the line is roughly seven miles upstream from the mouth. Mature females can be huge and seeing a twenty pound fish rolling in three feet of water will make your heart pound! Large flies that imitate baitfish and eels are used with success. Plugs and poppers on the surface are also effective and offer tremendous excitement. The fish then move up the river and can be found right up to the dam. A few are carried over the dam by the fish lift, but it is not a strong upriver run like the shad. Later in the year during the colder months, stripers and wipers can be found near the Peach Bottom plant's warm water discharge.

Another member of the "temperate bass" family is the white perch. (They are called "temperate" because they prefer temperate water— 65-75°F for stripers, 75-80°F for white perch). While most of the white perch in the river are not very large, they are strong and aggressive feeders. They also run in schools, so if you find one, you will often find more. I have frequently found these fish at the edges of mid-stream weed beds where the current was not very strong. Great sport can be had using small poppers for these fish with a light rod. Small plugs and spinners also work well. White perch can live in fresh, brackish, or salt water. Typically, they are found in the lower stretches of the river near the bay.

Channel Catfish

If you think catfish are just scavengers, you are in for a surprise. You will catch these fish now and then with plugs, jigs, and minnow-imitating lures. When I pulled up my first cat, I was also struck with the beauty of the silver-gray body and forked tail. Channel cats are found throughout the river, but become a preferred target for fly-fishermen when they feed on the surface. Many of the river's fish come to feed on the surface in August during the prolific white fly hatch. Smallmouth, panfish, and cats all gorge on this high density meal. Catfish can sometimes be found in eddies cleaning up the large numbers of dead adult mayflies (called spinners). They simply open their mouth and skim the surface, like a whale feeding on krill! Add your fly to the pile and you're likely to be into some excitement. Catfish are known as cavity spawners and like an enclosed space to lay their eggs. In some areas, boxes are put on the river bottom for this purpose. Channel cats can get very large – up to twenty pounds or more. Typical fish are one to five pounds.

Muskellunge

This big predator is a bit of a mystery. They are found in most portions of the river, but are only occasionally caught. It is usually by someone who is fishing for something else. Muskellunge tend to inhabit large pools off the main current of the river and feed primarily on small to medium-sized fish. They are "ambush predators" which lay waiting for their food and strike when it swims by. Large plugs or flies fished in these areas may put you into the battle of a lifetime. Keep the lure moving quickly and if a fish starts to follow, speed up. These fish can exceed four feet in length and have teeth to match so use a wire leader and stout tackle. Muskies look very similar to northern pike in appearance, but there are no pike in the Susquehanna so confusion about the identity of this fish is unlikely. The musky is not native to the Susquehanna, but is stocked by the Pennsylvania Fish and Boat Commission. Optimum fishing periods occur in the Spring and Fall, with Fall usually being preferred.

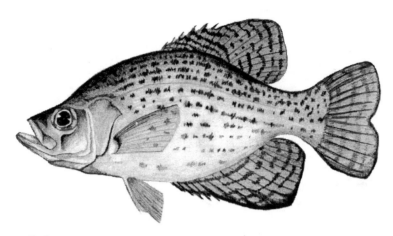

Panfish

Several types of sunfish and crappies inhabit the floodwaters of the dams. These fish are not typically very large, but they're not usually hard to catch, either. I think sunfish are a great way to introduce fly fishing to an angler because simple poppers produce exciting results. The fish are forgiving of casting imperfections and are not shy. Most sunfish and bluegills are found near structure in the lake-like sections, but a few will venture in the moving water of the river proper. These fish will attack many baits, but small spinners and dry flies or poppers are consistent producers.

Crappies live in schools and are aggressive minnow feeders. They will follow schools of baitfish in the impoundment areas of the river. Crappies prefer a lake-like habitat, but are not as linked to the structure as sunfish. The drawing above is a black crappie.

Rock bass are found in both the flowing and impounded portions of the river. True to its name, it is often found near rocks or other structure. It may look like a young smallmouth, but it has a bold red eye and a more prominent spot on the edge of the gill cover. Smaller poppers and spinners are usually effective for this fish.

Even for the veteran angler, it can be a fun way to spend the day, especially if other fish aren't biting.

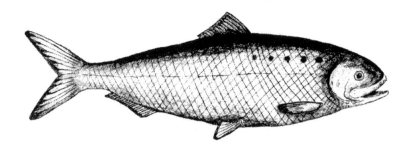

American Shad and Hickory Shad

Early in our country's history, the American shad was an important food resource. Settlers valued the fish enough to start the small but lengthy Yankee-Pennamite or Shad war over the rights to the fish. Sadly, neither side seemed much interested in preserving the fish for future generations. In many cases, the pioneers kept as many fish as the available salt supply could preserve. In the early days, it is believed that shad migrated over 640 miles from the sea to the headwaters near Binghamton, New York − not to mention their migratory eating habits which we'll talk about in a minute. Excessive harvest and small dams for agricultural or milling purposes caused some declines in the fishery, but the real damage came in 1830 when canal system dams closed off the river above Columbia. Many miles of stream habitat were lost. Luckily, these dams were abandoned and breached when railroads replaced the canal system. Shad populations recovered somewhat, but coal mining began degrading water quality and growing population centers added sewage and industrial waste.

As early as 1866 the first legislation was passed to ensure fish passage on the Susquehanna, but early efforts were not consistent or effective. Heavy fishing continued and exceeded a million fish per year for the State of Maryland in 1896. The shad fishery continued into the early 20th century, but plummeted after the construction of the Holtwood Dam (river mile 25) in 1910. Primitive fish passage and loss of prime habitat ended the huge runs of shad on the Susquehanna. The fishery was closed by 1920. In 1928, the Conowingo Dam was built without fish passage − a public acknowledgement that we had given up on this magnificent fish.

During the 1950s and 60s discussion started about restoring shad runs to the Susquehanna. Fish passage technology had improved and some habitat was still suitable. A better understanding of the shad life cycle also contributed to this optimism.

The shad is an anadromous fish. Anadromous means that, like the salmon, shad spend most of their adult lives in the ocean, but spawn in fresh water. Adults travel from their home stream to the Bay of Fundy area of the North Atlantic to feed on the rich plankton that exist there. After building strength and size, they return to freshwater to spawn. Some fish return to their natal stream, but others are found in rivers far from where they were born. Shad spawning is primarily triggered off of temperature which is optimally near 65°F. This turns out to be April or May in the Susquehanna and often coincides with the blooming of the white "shad bush" or juneberry found in the region. The actual spawning takes place at night from about nine to midnight. The fish swim together and the eggs are released into the current. There is no nest such as with bass or salmon. Typical spawning female fish are four to five years old and produce 100,000 to 300,000 eggs. Males are typically a year younger. Adults typically weigh three to eight pounds with occasional larger fish up to 12 pounds. Unlike many Pacific salmon, the shad can return to spawn several times, especially in the northern portions of its range including the Susquehanna.

After the eggs hatch, the young fish stay in the river until fall when a rain will often trigger the tiny fish to migrate downstream. Migration occurs before the water temperature drops below 40°F. There are many predators and several hydroelectric turbines to face on the journey and many don't survive. If they do, they migrate north and repeat the cycle.

Okay, back to the restoration effort. The population of shad in the river was very low up through the early 1970s. To avoid eliminating the fish altogether, the power utility company (PECO) financed a hatchery and a fish lift to allow some fish to get above the dam and spawn. Starting in 1972, the fish lift began operating at Conowingo, but initial returns were so small that shad from other areas including the Hudson River in New York and the Columbia River in Oregon were needed to supplement. The fish in the Columbia are believed to be the result of early transplants of Hudson River fish to the Sacramento River in California. The fish have spread as far north as Alaska on their own!

Although the shad populations did not initially respond very well, the biologists and companies persevered. By the early eighties, the shad were starting to return and the hydroelectric dams were simultaneously up for re-licensing with the Federal Energy Regulatory Commission. In 1984, a unique combination of utility companies, environmentalists, and fisheries agencies reached an agreement on a long term plan to provide fish passage on all four dams on the lower river.

Today, fish lifts are running at each of the three lower dams and migrating fish have been verified at the two new upper lifts starting in 1997. A final lift is planned to be in operation at the York Haven dam by April of the year 2000. The hickory shad, alewife, and blueback herring will also benefit from the restoration. Eels and striped bass may also use the passage facilities to some degree.

The future has not looked brighter for the shad for nearly a hundred years. Recent data indicates that not only is the shad run increasing, but the proportion of wild fish is increasing as well. The stage is set for a steady, sustainable return of this spectacular fish. It has been a long and difficult road to rebuilding the strength of the American shad, but it is exactly the kind of perseverant, cooperative effort that is required to manage the shared resources that our rivers represent.

Assuming that the restoration will be successful and allow sportfishing to return, shad can be caught on a variety of small flies and lures. Spin-fishermen use darts (a small jig), spinners, and small spoons, often trolled or just held steady in the current. During the spring spawning run, the fish tend to be in tight schools. If you find a shad, there are probably more nearby.

American Shad Adults Returning to the Susquehanna

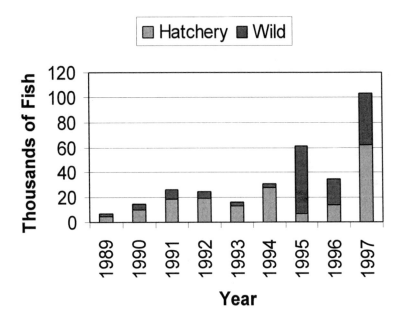

Fly-fishermen use small, brightly colored flies to catch shad. They can be drifted or held in the current above a known pod of fish.

The principal physical differences between the two species of shad are size and mouth structure. The hickory shad is smaller, typically weighing one to three pounds compared to three to eight pounds for the American shad. A more definitive way to discern the two is to close the mouth of the fish and determine if the lower jaw extends past the upper. If it does, it is a hickory shad. A final important difference, both for the restoration and sportfishing, is that the hickory shad spawns in feeder creeks while the American shad stays in the main river.

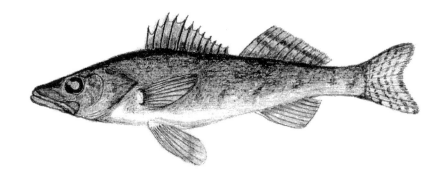

Walleye

Walleye are found throughout much of the river, and are probably the second most popular target for sport fishermen. The walleye does not typically fight and jump as much as the smallie and does not usually take surface lures which are very exciting to fish. Despite all of this, walleye are deemed desirable by many because they make superb eating.

With the exception of surface plugs and flies, walleye can be caught on many of the same lures as smallmouth and are often caught by accident by smallmouth fisherman using jigs, spinners, spoons, or plugs. Walleye are aggressive minnow feeders and imitations of the local baitfish are a good place to start. Walleyes are sometimes found in groups, so continue working an area where you find one.

Walleyes spawn in the early Spring. They are broadcast spawners and prefer gravel or cobble to distribute the eggs. The walleye season is closed during this time since reproductive success is limited. The Pennsylvania Fish and Boat Commission also stocks millions of walleye in the river each year.

The best time to fish for walleye is typically in the Fall and Winter. The unusual looking glassy eye that gives the walleye its name is very sensitive to light, so bright light is to be avoided. This fish also prefers cooler water, so the cold, overcast days of the late season are often the best fishing.

Many people fish for walleyes near the base of dams and the mouth of tributaries where baitfish may be found. Typical sizes are ten to twenty inches, but larger specimens up to ten pounds are caught.

General Tackle

Some of your fishing gear will be the same regardless of your choice of rod and reel. We'll start at the bottom and work our way up.

The Susquehanna can be an excellent place for wading because of the good access and many shallow, rocky areas. Many people wade with just an old pair of sneakers in the summer when the water is warm. Even then, a pair of felt-soled shoes or cleats will provide a better grip on the often slippery rocks. Early or late in the year, waders are needed to protect you from the chilly water. Standard waders are adequate for most times, but four or five mm thick neoprene is excellent for really cold fishing. Unfortunately, I find thicker neoprene is too hot and sticky for much of the rest of the year on the Susquehanna because I cover quite a bit of ground on foot while fishing. Thinner neoprene (two or three mm) is available and will provide some relief.

A simple vest with a few items will make your fishing more enjoyable. A pair of narrow-nosed pliers are a great aid for crushing hook barbs and quickly unhooking fish. Crushing the barb causes less damage to the fish and the pliers allow you to quickly grasp the hook without worrying about teeth or getting hooked yourself. I use a hemostat with a curved tip and this works superbly for unhooking, but is a bit weak for crushing larger barbs. Standard narrow-nose pliers are better for this, but you can do this task before heading out if you are diligent. A pair of fingernail clippers for trimming line instead of using your teeth will also keep your dentist happier. I find a stream thermometer a useful tool, especially if you take advantage of the warm water discharge areas during the colder months. Finally, a hook hone or file will result in fewer lost fish if you remember to sharpen hooks frequently. A hook is really sharp when it passes this test: after sharpening, drag the point over your fingernail with only enough pressure to hold on to the hook. If it starts to dig in, it's sharp. If not, get back to work.

For some flies or lures, additional weight may be necessary to get down to fish near the bottom. Historically, fishermen have used lead for this purpose because it is soft, heavy, and easily melted. Unfortunately, it is also toxic to most life including birds and humans. It has been recently documented that ducks, geese and loons are ingesting lead and dying in some areas. The birds naturally pick up small stones and grit to aid digestion and lead is picked up by accident. Although this is usually due to hunter's shot, we all need to do our part to reduce toxic materials in the environment. Fishermen's weights are now also being made from tin, which is essentially non-toxic. Tin is also soft and easily melted, but not quite as dense. Your weight may be a tad larger, but is less harmful to the environment.

Polarized sunglasses are essential for spotting fish and underwater cover. Many people feel that amber is the best all-around lens color. However, if you can afford two pair, then dark gray or green for bright days and amber or yellow for overcast days will increase your ability to spot structure and fish underwater. A brimmed hat, sunscreen, and insect repellent (in summer) will round out your gear.

In addition to your actual equipment, there are two simple concepts to "bring along" that will help you catch more fish. Remember that fish face into the current. This means you should generally work your way upstream so that you approach the fish from behind and debris that you dislodge while wading will be carried away from the fish.

Also remember to avoid spooking fish by wading quietly. Use obstructions such as rocks, logs, and weed beds to hide your silhouette and break up the waves you make while wading. Fish are sensitive to pressure waves in the water using their lateral line. If they can't see you and your wave motion is slight or blocked, you can often sneak to within a few feet of rising fish. Watching a surface strike up close is one of the greatest joys of fishing.

Fly-fishing

The recent surge in fly-fishing popularity has brought many more fly casters to the Susquehanna. Smallmouth bass, in particular, are aggressive feeders and spectacular sport with a fly rod.

There is some debate about the optimum outfit to use on the Susquehanna. Because of the many smaller trout streams in the area, lots of folks have a five or six weight system with a double taper or weight-forward floating line. If you do, go ahead and give it a try on the bigger river. Some people never move away from this type of gear since it provides superior sport with smaller fish. Other river experts believe that an eight weight rod with a weight-forward line is better for casting larger flies for larger fish, particularly in the windy conditions often found on the tremendous width of the Susquehanna.

Perhaps a good quality seven weight would be the best all-around rod. Rod length is again a matter of taste, but something between eight and nine feet will serve you well. In the slower backwaters or strong deep currents of the river, some anglers use a sinking or sink tip line to get down. Alternatively, a small piece of shot or Deepwater Express® can be attached to the line. Casting does require some adjustment, but this type of rig may be necessary if the water is too cold or deep for surface activity.

Unless the water is very low and clear, seven to nine foot leader lengths are adequate. Fine tippets are not generally necessary. I would generally not recommend going below a four to six pound tippet strength. River fish like the smallmouth often strike quite savagely and smaller tippets may leave you holding nothing at all.

Standard single-action reels are generally adequate unless you are chasing stripers or muskies. In this case, a heavier duty reel with a disc drag may be helpful. Finally, I suggest that hook barbs be flattened to minimize damage to the fish.

Food Sources in the Susquehanna

The river is rich in food sources which can be categorized into three important groups: 1) Crayfish , 2) Baitfish , and 3) Insects and their larvae.

1) Crayfish

There are many species of crayfish, but they all look fairly similar. They range in color from reddish to brown to olive which varies with their environment and life stage. Look for them meandering between the rocks in search of food. Crayfish are an important found source for smallmouth bass, particularly in the summer and fall. They escape their enemies with a flick of their tail, which propels them backward out of danger. Imitations should be fished accordingly by either a steady retrieve near the bottom or a twitched retrieve at various depths. Effective imitations can be seen in the photos.

2) Baitfish

There are many types of small fish that larger predators forage on. Unlike the crayfish, however, the distinctions here are often important. Sculpins are an important group. These are small bottom feeding fish that are brown, olive or black, and have prominent pectoral fins which stick out to the sides. An imitation of this fish is visible in the third row of the fly collection. These fish live down in the rocks and artificials should be worked there, too. The key to successful fishing here is to replicate the natural activity of this bait– swimming or darting between the rocks or weeds near the bottom.

Many species make up the more conventional looking minnows including shiners, chubs, dace, and juvenile fish. There are variations here as well, but many of them can be imitated with versions of the Clouser Deep Minnow. The inventor of this fly is Bob Clouser, a lifelong Susquehanna valley resident and serious river advocate. The chartreuse/white Deep Minnow may be the most important fly in your box.

3) Insects

There are several key insects for gamefish of the Susquehanna. Possibly the most important is larvae of the dobsonfly, called a hellgrammite. It's not a pretty name, but then it's not a pretty insect. The larval form is a dark grub-like creature with nasty pincers for capturing other aquatic insects for food. Nonetheless, it is a significant part of the food supply for smallmouth bass. The adult insect is also found after hatching out and flying or climbing onto the vegetation near the bank. Fishing a black Woolly Bugger with a slow stripping motion over rocks or weed beds where hellgrammites live will often attract fish.

In August, an evening-hatching mayfly known as the white fly (Ephoron leukon) is seen in certain parts of the river in such tremendous numbers that it appears to be snowing. During these intense events, many of the gamefish of the river come up to the surface for dinner. A white or cream colored dry fly will produce at these times. Trophy hunters use imitations of small fish to lure out monsters feeding on the juveniles which are feeding on the mayflies. Talk about a food chain in action!

Terrestrial insects such as grasshoppers and ants are also plentiful in the summer and early fall. Imitations fished near the bank will produce bass and panfish.

Other aquatic insects such as mayflies and caddisflies are locally abundant. The best strategy is to capture an adult and/or a nymph with a small net and tie on a similar or slightly larger imitation. Often forgotten foods are the nymphs of the dragonfly and damselfly. These are hearty meals for many fish and should be given a try.

Flies shown in photo:
First row: damselfly nymph, parachute style light Cahill (white fly imitation), tent-wing caddis. Second row: dragonfly nymph, weedless deer-hair popper. Third row: grasshopper, bead-head Woolly Bugger. Fourth row: popper, Zonker. Fifth row: crayfish, chamois leech. Sixth row: sculpin, Clouser Deep Minnow®

Spinning

Modern spinning tackle includes a well-balanced reel, a graphite or composite rod, and quality monofilament line. I prefer a seven to eight foot rod made from a graphite/polymer composite, but personal preference plays a big role in the selection. In any case, remember that longer rods of equal stiffness give you better casting capability, but overall balance of the rod, reel and line is critical. Composite rods are lightweight, reasonably priced, and fairly tough. Fiberglass rods are more durable, but somewhat heavier and less sensitive. You may still want one if you are real tough on equipment or are looking for something for the kids. High end graphite rods are extremely sensitive, but you pay a penalty in cost and durability.

Open-face spinning reels have improved a great deal to the point where they are the only non-fly-fishing type I use. Look for a wide diameter, flared spool which aids in casting lighter lures. Some of the newer reels have a trigger on the bail which allows one-handed casting. This is a worthwhile feature if well designed.

Generally, drag mechanisms set in the front are preferable because the discs are bigger and operate more smoothly. Also note the number of bearings that support the shaft. More is usually better, since it spreads out the load. If possible, check to see if wear parts such as gears, bearings, and the bail return tab are made of metal or plastic.

Typically, the metal will last longer. Finally, take the reel, flip the bail, and slowly turn the crank to the point where the bail will flip back. This action should be smooth and not get stuck or require large effort to get the bail over the return tab.

Six or eight pound test monofilament is recommended for most fishing. Learn how to tie an improved clinch knot and always wet the line a bit as you cinch it down. This keeps the line from weakening due to the heat caused by the friction of pulling the knot tight. Also remember to use a barrel swivel if you use a lure that can spin such as a spoon.

Most conditions won't require a leader, but sunny days and low water may require a three or four pound leader. A blood knot or surgeon's knot can be used to attach the leader to the main line. Some folks enjoy using an ultra light outfit with four pound test line all the time. This is a blast for smaller fish, but you'll be more likely to come home with a great story than a trophy fish. One final note on spinning tackle is that I strongly recommend the use of artificial lures only and crushing the barbs on your hooks. Most of the fish you catch should be returned to the river with as little harm as possible and this is very difficult if you use live bait. Simply put, the fish tend to swallow bait and unhooking them becomes tough. Live bait is unnecessary since most of the game fish in the river will readily strike at many imitations. With any lure, crushed barbs will allow unhooking with less damage to the fish and may help you land more fish because of easier hook penetration. Use of live minnows has also accidentally introduced detrimental exotic species into many lakes and rivers, and should be avoided or at least determined to be native species.

There are many effective spinning lures. A representative selection is visible in the photo. On the surface, poppers and floating plugs are effective for bass. Diving plugs called crankbaits such as the "Bomber" shown also work well. There are also several classes of lures that work strictly below the surface. The classic bladed spinner will catch nearly all kinds of gamefish if worked slowly near the bottom. Spoons are similar, but remember to always use a swivel since they generate more line twist. Last but not least are jigs. This versatile type of lure can be tipped with fur, hair, plastic, or other materials. The heavy head gets the imitation down near the bottom quickly and can be twitched or hopped during the retrieve to stimulate strikes.

Spinning Lures Shown in photo:
Top Row: Plastic Sculpin, Shad Dart
Second row: Rapala® Minnow, Spoon
Third row: Rebel Crawfish®, Super Vibrax® spinner
Fourth row: Bomber A®, Plastic Worm

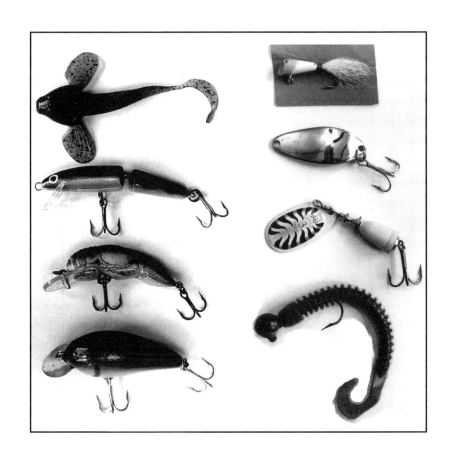

Chapter Three

The Susquehanna Valley on Foot

Hiking the many trails, bluffs, and islands of the river valley is a great way to enjoy the countryside. Before you go, there are a few preparations that will make your journey a lot more enjoyable.

The single most important item is footwear. Striking off into the woods in your running shoes is good for neither you or the shoes. The best thing to do is to get yourself a good pair of hiking boots. There is a tremendous variety available, but certain features will be the most relevant. Nearly all the footwear offered to hikers today has adequate support for your ankle, but there is at least one notable exception. Newer shoes offered by running shoe companies have a lug-like sole for traction, but are low cut similar to a running shoe. While these are attractive because of their low weight, I would avoid them if you are new to hiking or have ever had trouble with turning your ankle. Uneven surfaces such as rocks and tree roots put a lot of strain on your lower legs. Assuming that you have found a high cut boot, lighter is generally better. Large, heavy boots used in mountaineering are not necessary and simply tire you out faster.

Another important characteristic of boots is waterproofness. Most boots are water resistant and will keep you dry through the occasional puddle. Few will do so if you are in the water steadily. Look for a boot that contains a Gore-Tex (® W.L. Gore) liner. This will keep water out all day. Gore-Tex is not heavy, but it is expensive.

Assuming your feet are happy, it's time to protect the rest of yourself from the elements. The main things to be mindful of are weather and bugs. You can hike some portions of the valley year-round, but remember to dress accordingly. Carrying extra layers of clothes and a light rain coat in a small pack is not a bad idea. You never know when an excursion might turn out to be a bit longer than intended.

One of the results of being near the bountiful Susquehanna is a healthy crop of insects. While they are great for the fish and birds nearby, they mostly pester humans. Always take or pre-apply a good repellent for hiking. The cool forest trails and backwaters of the river are a haven for mosquitoes. Forgetting it can ruin an otherwise enjoyable hike.

Another optional item is a field guide or two. I enjoy labeling and learning about everything as I go. For trees or birds, I highly recommend the Peterson Field Guides®. The excellent illustrations and logical organization avoid a lot of frustration. For birds, you also need a pair of binoculars. I suggest the best pair you can afford. In other words, you get what you pay for. Higher quality optics gather light better and show color more accurately. For birding, 7x or 8x magnification is optimum. Higher powers are difficult to hold steady enough for enjoyable viewing.

Now you're ready, but where do you go? Let's take a quick trip upriver to highlight some of the best spots. Just north of Havre de Grace is Susquehanna State Park which provides forest hiking trails as well as good access to the river for launching boats. Just upriver from the park is the Shures Landing Wildflower area. This 1.75 mile stretch of river flood plain has a trail with many of the area's wildflowers and woodland birds. The Mason-Dixon Trail also follows the Susquehanna for many miles on or near the west bank. Detailed trail desrciptions and maps are available from Mason-Dixon Trail System, Inc. at 719 Oakbourne Rd., West Chester, PA 19382-7509.

Crossing to the east side of the river at Conowingo Dam, there is a parking area and trail to Funks Pond. It's a nice hike and you can fish when you get there!

Susquehannock State Park is just north of Drumore and has a rock outcropping with an incredible view of the river. It is also a good place for birding during the fall migration. Many birds of prey and others fly the river corridor. Hiking, birding and picnicking are also good in the rest of the park.

Just upstream lies the Holtwood Dam area. There are two promontories with excellent views. Face Rock Overlook allows you to view the dam and all of the hardware associated with a hydroelectric facility. The view at Pinnacle Overlook is less disrupted by power lines and transformers, but the river is more lake-like behind the dam. Trails of all lengths are available in this area ranging from the short loops at Pinnacle Overlook to cross-country tracks such as the Conestoga and Mason-Dixon. There is also a wildflower area at Shenk's Ferry. North of Columbia is Chickie's Rock State Park. The park is rather unique in that it is a popular rock climbing area. On warm weekend days, you'll see several teams ascending the steep front face. Get proper instruction and equipment before joining them! There is also nice hiking in the area and a nice view from the lookout.

While not a "wilderness experience", the river greenway on the east bank of downtown Harrisburg provides a good model of how a river can be an asset to a city. Many hikers, bikers and fishermen enjoy access to a good stretch of river here.

The Fort Hunter area is not big enough for serious hiking, but has room for picnicking and fishing. Its most unique feature is that many of the trees in the park have placards for those who are trying to learn.

Shikellamy State Park near Sunbury has two parts and is a fun place to explore. There is a bluff on the west side of the river that has an incredible view of the junction between the West Branch of the Susquehanna and the main river. It's a great spot for a picnic. There is also Packers Island near the forks that has more room for hiking, bicycling, or fishing.

Another way to enjoy hiking in the valley is by combining it with boating. There are many publicly owned islands in the Susquehanna, but the stretch from Sunbury to Harrisburg is especially good for this. There is even an effort underway to create "river trails" that highlight these opportunities. Please respect islands that are closed for nesting or are private property.

Chapter Four

A Boating Primer for the Susquehanna

Because of the wide variety of conditions found on the Susquehanna, you'll see everything from float tubes to house boats while out on the river. Many of the larger craft, however, are confined to the lake-like regions behind the large dams. The main reasons for this are the swift current and shallow rocky bottom found in the more riverine stretches.

No matter which boat you use, you must be prepared for the possibility of "swamping." This means a life jacket for every person in the boat. Recently, the rules changed such that the "seat cushion" style of floatation device is no longer acceptable in Pennsylvania. Wearable vest (type IV) floatation devices are now required.

There are several classes of water craft that are suitable for nearly all of the river. These include canoes, inflatables, and jonboats. The ancient and venerable canoe has been around for a long time for good reason — it is inexpensive and versatile.

There are many styles and sizes available, but there are a few rules to keep in mind.

Unless you plan to use the canoe alone (which I don't recommend), I suggest a canoe of about fifteen to seventeen feet. Smaller boats are available, but it gets crowded quickly if you carry much gear or a dog. Canoes larger than this are typically heavier and more expensive, but useful for multiple day boat trips.

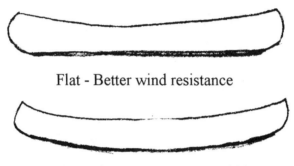

Flat - Better wind resistance

Curved - Better maneuverability

Canoe   Profiles

The next important parameter of the canoe is the hull shape. Narrow canoes are faster but more likely to get you wet due to a disbalanced fisherman or a sudden squall. Wider canoes have a couple advantages — not only are they more stable, they also have a shallower draft. This means you are less likely to run aground in shallow areas. The main advantage to the narrower canoe is that it is faster, since it presents less surface area to cause drag in the water. The important width to remember is at the waterline, not at the gunwales. Depth is also important since it plays a role in carrying capacity, wind cross-section, and the ability to shed water splashed up from rapids. Unless you plan multi-day adventures, the wind factor is probably the most important on most of the Susquehanna. Most of the rapids are mild or avoidable.

Two other characteristics are important to the handling characteristics of a canoe. Looking at a canoe from the side will tell you a lot about how it will respond to current and wind. A very flat keel or bottom from fore to aft will result in a craft that is resistant to blowing around in the wind, but not very maneuverable in tight situations. On the Susquehanna, wind resistance is likely to be more important.

Canoe Cross-Sections

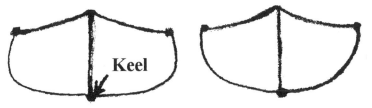

Higher Stability   **Higher Maneuverability**

The end view of the canoe makes the second feature more visible. The keel protrudes down from the bottom of the boat. The larger it is, the more the boat will tend to track straight ahead. This means that more keel results in better wind resistance, but lower mobility in whitewater.

The last big decision with a canoe is hull material. There are a few wood and/or canvas canoes still around, but they should be avoided. Unless, of course, the wood "feel" is important to you and you don't mind a lot of sanding and re-finishing to avoid rotting. A more practical choice is a modern polymeric material. Many of these are available with wood trim, which gives the boat a nice feel. Various "plastics" are molded to shape and are durable and reasonably priced. Others are built up from resin and fiber reinforcing. This is commonly called fiberglass and is strong, but brittle. A sharp collision or blow can cause cracking or make a hole. A special version of this construction method uses Kevlar® fibers and a special resin. These hulls are very strong and about 25% lighter than fiberglass, but cost on the order of twice as much for an otherwise similar canoe.

Other polymer-based hulls are more compliant. Royalex® is an excellent example of a modern hull material. It is a composite of several layers. The outer layer is vinyl for abrasion and UV resistance. Under this material is a layer of ABS plastic which is strong but compliant. The core is a unicellular foam that provides stiffness and flotation. Together, the hull is an excellent combination of light weight, strength, and durability. Other similar composites that use polyethylene or polycarbonate are also used by leading manufacturers.

Another benefit to the plastic hull is that it is quiet. This is especially important while fishing and adds to your peace and solitude at any time. In contrast, aluminum canoes are loud when the paddle hits the gunwale and when you slide over rocks in shallow water. Aluminum canoes also tend to stick on rocks more than other materials. Finally, they feel rather cold compared to the polymer hull. Despite these drawbacks, they may still be a good choice if you want an extremely tough canoe.

A few final words about canoes before we move on. Special brackets to mount an electric trolling motor are available. There are even square-sterned canoes designed for adding a motor. I generally prefer the exercise, but motors can be nice for getting back upstream to where you put in.

As mentioned before, all canoes can be tipped. I don't believe that any small craft belongs out in the middle of a huge reservoir. Storms and squalls can put you into trouble too quickly. Although the Susquehanna is not generally a difficult river to navigate, beware of hazards such as weirs, dams, and trees. Practice in quiet water and learn good technique first.

Canoes (and other boats) are more fun with a few generic items. A "dry bag" is a waterproof pouch with a roll up top that will protect things like cameras and lunches. This is useful on all trips since the side-to-side paddling action drips water in the boat. An anchor is a good addition for stopping mid-stream for fishing, pictures, etc.

The next class of boat is the very popular "jonboat." These are wide, flat, shallow craft used primarily as fishing platforms.

They are less tolerant of rough water than canoes, but are more stable for standing and casting. These boats are also available with aluminum or plastic hulls. They are easily rowed or motorized with either a small outboard or electric trolling motor, and reasonably priced. Jonboats are similar to canoes in size, but typically a bit shorter because the wide beam creates more room. Twelve to sixteen foot lengths are recommended for a pair of fishermen and their gear. Look for a width of four feet or more on the bottom of the boat for the best stability.

Jonboat with motor

A couple of other notes about motors. Many experienced boaters put a shield around the motor propeller to protect it from rocks, heavy weeds, and other hazards. This can save a lot of money and hassle, especially with an outboard. As an alternative, jet outboards are now available. With this technology, the propeller is replaced with a water jet. The conversion is somewhat costly and reduces the available horsepower, but the result is robust for river duty. Lastly, if you do decide to get a non-electric motor, please buy a four-cycle as opposed to a two-cycle motor. Although they are a bit more expensive, they are much quieter and much less polluting. Think of the cost as an investment in environmental protection!

Inflatable raft with trolling motor

Inflatable boats are a relatively new group. These range from scaled-up bathtub toys to the now famous Zodiac used by Jacques Cousteau and his crew in the open ocean. Not everyone takes these boats seriously, but there are some nice craft out there.

The simplest inflatable is the float tube. There has been an explosion of popularity in the float tube since it was discovered to be an excellent fishing platform, particularly in smaller waters. Caddis and other manufacturers have made them very comfortable, even for extended periods of time. The feeling reminds me of a floating lounge chair. The fishing can be almost as comfortable. The one exception is that unlike the easy chair, you usually want to move around a bit in the tube to fish or visit various spots. The only practical way to do so is by paddling with fins over your wading shoes. So, although it is relaxing, float tube fishing is not for the lazy. The legs get a workout if you're out for very long. Some areas of the river are also too shallow for tubing, since your "draft" is roughly the inseam of your pant leg. In these areas, careful wading or a canoe probably make more sense. One advantage of float tubes is cost- an entire setup can cost as little as $200 including $100 or so for neoprene waders. I have used a tube in the Susquehanna, but it's not my favorite way to go since fast water, submerged hazards, or power boats in some areas can make river tubing rather dangerous. Wading, paddling (with a paddle instead of fins), or an electric-powered craft are the best fit for me.

The next step up in the inflatable world is probably the canoe or kayak. These still have the advantages of low cost and portability, but cannot generally be motorized or provide the stability of a jonboat or flat-bottomed canoe. In addition, they suffer from another problem common to nearly all inflatables which is susceptibility to wind. Because they present a large cross-sectional area to the wind with little or no keel, they tend to blow around too easily.

Inflatable rafts are the most diverse group. Some are simply a single chamber of thin-walled vinyl. Others include many excellent features such as rigid flooring with keels, motor mounts, multi-chamber design, oarlocks, and even windshields. Most of these features are self-explanatory, but the chamber design can be more subtle. Make sure that the multiple chambers form concentric structures like the raft shown on the right. This way, if one chamber gets punctured, the raft will still float. Other designs such as those on the left will probably NOT stay afloat if you lose one chamber. I have fished from an inflatable for many years and never punctured the hull with a hook. I did get a hole from my Labrador pup when she was teething. Thankfully, the raft was in the backyard at the time.

There are many other types of boats including semi-vees, "bass boats", "ski boats", sailboats, and more. Most of these are less suitable for the shallow, rocky, riverine portions of the Susquehanna because their draft is too deep. They will run aground and be damaged (or at least get stuck) too often. You will see many of these boats in the deeper, calmer backwater areas behind dams.

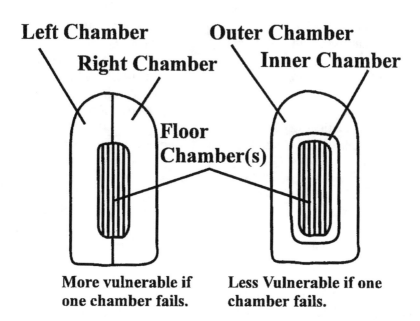

Left Chamber **Outer Chamber**

Right Chamber **Inner Chamber**

Floor Chamber(s)

More vulnerable if one chamber fails.   Less Vulnerable if one chamber fails.

Chapter Five

River Stewardship

The Susquehanna is a tremendous resource for all of us to enjoy. The beauty and life it has today is a testament to its resiliency. For the past couple hundred years we have appreciated the river primarily by dumping, damming, and diverting it to suit our needs. Fortunately, the last couple of decades have shown some promise in turning this trend around. Anti-pollution laws and better environmental awareness have allowed the river to cleanse itself to some degree. There is still much to do and the river needs every one of us as a friend on its side. There are several things that each of us can do to help improve the quality of the river corridor and subsequently our experiences on it. Get involved!

Be politically "green"

It may seem like a long way from the voting booth to the boat ramp, but it's not. Our elected officials have a great deal of influence in how our rivers and other resources are managed. Read your local paper before the election and find out who has a track record of protecting resources. There are also a number a public officials that are very important, although not elected by the public. The Susquehanna River Basin Commission and the Pennsylvania Fish and Boat Commission are critical "managers," and our experiences on the river will be greatly affected by the policies they create. There are often opportunities to comment on proposed policies, and we all owe it to ourselves and the river to make sure a conservation agenda is heard.

Join conservation and river watch groups

The Susquehanna is a huge watershed made up of many small and medium-sized streams. Local groups have a great deal of power in determining the quality of the water that they add to the river. Water resource councils and commissions make decisions about water treatment, industrial permitting, land use and other issues affecting the river. Many of these groups are staffed by local people, including volunteers. Having river advocates on these councils is important. Otherwise, the only agenda forwarded may not protect the river's integrity. Other groups, such as the Susquehanna Smallmouth Alliance and The Chesapeake Bay Foundation have specific and worthwhile goals which may fit your individual interests.

Use water wisely

Although the Susquehanna is large, it is finite. A growing population is placing a greater consumptive demand on the river. Water that is removed from the river and lost to evaporation or other mechanisms is said to be consumptive. Less water not only means less habitat in the river, it also disturbs the entire Upper Chesapeake Bay ecosystem which depends on the large flow of fresh water from the Susquehanna to remain primarily fresh. Many salt-intolerant creatures and plants that historically thrived in the Upper Bay are struggling partially due to lower fresh water flows and subsequent higher salinity. We are all part of the problem and the solution. There are several ways we can reduce our water consumption:

1)Landscape with plants that don't require supplemental water.

2)If you grow food plants, use efficient irrigation like drip systems. Water early in the morning to reduce evaporation loss.

3)If you have a lawn, cut it higher to reduce evaporation.

4)Use low-flow showerheads, faucets, and appliances. Make sure your systems don't leak.

5)Always use a shut-off nozzle on the garden hose. Five or more gallons a minute can be lost through an unchecked hose.

6)Always turn off the faucet while you brush your teeth or wash the dishes.

Catch and Release

There are just too many fishermen hauling stringers of fish out of the river. It's simple — if we keep it up, we'll have nothing but small numbers of small fish to catch. Keeping the largest fish is particularly harmful. For instance, a four year old female striped bass lays about 65,000 eggs. Nine years later, if she avoids all the nets and hooks after her, she'll weigh forty pounds and lay nearly 5,000,000 eggs. She is a hundred times more valuable to her species now. It's difficult not to keep such a prize, but she is our future.

One excellent substitute is photographs. Do not exhaust the fish while fighting it (particularly stripers). Unhook it in the water (not on the bank or boat), and then briefly raise the fish to snap the shot. Resuscitate the fish as much as necessary by gently moving it back and forth in the water while supporting it in an upright position. This may take several minutes or more. Eventually, it will swim off under its own power. For me, it is a great feeling to know the fish I catch can return to the river to help keep the ecosystem in balance and maybe even be caught again someday.

On a similar note, photos are a great way to capture wildflowers, too. The fragile blossoms won't last long if picked and no one else can enjoy them once you remove them.

Protecting Susquehanna water quality

Many of the household chemicals that we use can be very harmful to river life. It is important to develop good habits at home that include the proper disposal of all substances such as paints, solvents, cleaners, lubricants, and fuels. Hydrocarbons such as gasoline and oil spread to form a thin suffocating film on the water they contaminate. A quart of oil can contaminate more than a million gallons of drinking water and suffocate aquatic life, so don't let it spill on the pavement where it will eventually end up in a storm drain that flows into the river. Finally, remember to recycle as much as possible and think about the materials you buy. Recycling saves energy and resources (often including water) and buying items with recycled content helps close the recycling loop. A gallon of recycled motor oil will return as about two quarts of fresh motor oil. Making that same two quarts from scratch would take forty-two gallons of crude and more energy.

Paper is of special interest because a lot of water is used to create it and the methods of production have very different environmental impacts. Much of the paper we use is still bleached with molecular (elemental) chlorine which results in chemical compounds harmful to most life, including humans. One important decision you can make is to use paper that is unbleached or peroxide bleached. Peroxide bleaching makes excellent white paper without the dangerous by-products. Look for labels that say TCF (totally chlorine free), SCF (secondarily chlorine free), or PCF (processed chlorine free). The ECF (elemental chlorine free) process still uses a chlorine-containing compound, but is better than the typical process.

Finally, there is the mundane but important matter of litter. Everywhere I go, I find it. The flood plains of the river have all kinds of trash strewn about by the power of the river. I have seen 55 gallon drums wedged in the tree branches ten feet over my head. Now I realize that it would be a tad inconvenient to drag home a full-sized drum to dispose of it properly. However, if you are out fishing with a vest or hiking with a pack, think about taking home MORE than you brought in. Aluminum cans are light, crushable, and a major waste if NOT recycled. Ninety-five percent of the energy used to create the can the first time is re-used when the can is recycled. Fishermen have to be particularly vigilant about proper disposal of knots of fishing line, lure packages, etc.

Land meets water

Perhaps you are lucky enough to live on or near the Susquehanna or one of its tributaries. In any case, we all live in a watershed. We must bear in mind that the land we caretake runs off into some stream, somewhere. Typical inorganic lawn fertilizers burden a waterway with excess nutrients that create algae which can choke the flow and consume precious oxygen when it dies back. Organic fertilizers are less concentrated which is advantageous because they are less likely to "burn" the grass from over application and are more likely to be absorbed locally.

Pesticides used to kill insects in your yard eventually wash down into the creeks and undermine the food chain by killing insects there, too. Many herbicides cause similar damage by killing the plants necessary to support the life in the stream. While I don't suspect we will eliminate these substances altogether, please think about why you are using a particular agent, what the alternatives are, and what the potential (downstream) impact might be. If your lawn is a bit more "biodiverse" than your neighbor's, wear it like a badge! Some areas should be used to propagate native grasses and other plants, too. Integrated Pest Management uses a methodology that includes a variety of techniques to maintain a balance in your yard and garden. Biological or organic pest control solutions such as purple martin houses and beneficial predatory insects are typically used instead of clouds of toxics filling the air. Finally, when there are no other alternatives, use the chemicals safely on a limited target. Protect yourself and think about how the substance will be absorbed into the world around you.

Similarly, supporting organic farmers in your area will help extend your good habits and reduce pesticide contamination of other land and water.

Boats and water quality

There are several ways that boats and boating can harm the Susquehanna, and we should work to minimize or eliminate these sources of degradation.

Boat and motor size and selection is the first order of business. If the river is the primary site for using your boat, it need not be large. Smaller boats are more efficient to transport and power. Unless you plan to fish the center of the large reservoirs, canoes and jonboats are an excellent choice. Small boats can often be human powered, which does not pollute the water and keeps you in shape! It is also quiet which is ideal for fishing and wildlife watching. Last but not least, smaller boats make smaller wakes which cause less bank erosion. Regardless of size, lower speeds will help reduce wakes which can damage the stream bank and stir up excessive silt.

Electric motors are the next step up in power and retain most of the quiet features of people power. They do require stored energy in the form of a battery, but are still less energy consumptive and less polluting than internal combustion engines.

Gasoline-based engines do provide the highest levels of power output and roaming range. They are the worst polluters, but are not all equal. Newer four-cycle engines are much less dirty and noisy than the two-cycle units that dominate the market. This is likely to change over time as the Environmental Protection Agency is considering legislation which would phase out two-cycle boat motors. Although the four-cycle engines cost and weigh a bit more, all of the boaters I know that have switched to them are very happy because of the lower noise and smoke. The river benefits in the long term, too.

If your boat is used in other waters, remember to keep it clean and dry when not in use. Washing the hull with non-toxic (no chlorine or phosphorus) cleaners and draining all of the compartments will help avoid the accidental transportation of exotic species into the watershed. Species such as the zebra mussel have caused a great deal of mechanical damage to pumps, motors, and turbines in the Great Lakes, and the environmental impact is still being assessed. Mussels are filter feeders and consume the plankton also needed by young fish. An adult mussel filters about a liter a day which really adds up due to the large beds these organisms form. The water may actually end up clearer, but may hold less food for native species. It is believed that these mussels were (and are) transported and introduced unknowingly by boat owners.

There are many more ways you can help improve water quality. More detailed information about these ideas and others are available from sources including your local extension service, the Chesapeake Bay Foundation, The Alliance for the Chesapeake Bay, soil conservation districts, and others. Most of these resources are free and we can use them to educate ourselves and work toward a future with healthier watersheds.

Chapter Six

The Chesapeake Bay to Port Deposit

The Susquehanna pours 24 billion gallons of water into the Chesapeake on a typical day. This water carries a massive sediment load which creates the huge extended delta known as the "Susquehanna flats." The water in this area is predominantly fresh, but the depth still varies with the tides. Extreme caution should be used when boating in this area since depths of a foot or less are common at low tide. Early spring brings striped bass into the lower Susquehanna and exciting fishing can be found as these fish roll in the shallow water.

Aerial view looking downstream into the Chesapeake Bay

47

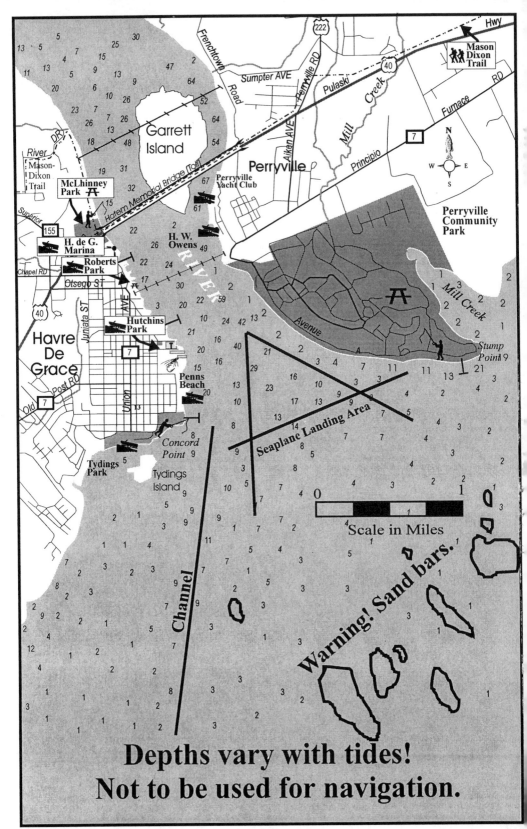

Depths vary with tides!
Not to be used for navigation.

The mouth of the river has a town on each side – Havre de Grace on the west bank and Perryville on the east. Havre de Grace has better access to the river and bay with multiple ramps and marinas. Perryville has a nice park for picnicking and bank fishing along with a set of factory outlet stores in town for times when you or your partner would rather be indoors.

Water depths actually increase as you get into the river proper, but it's still a good idea to watch for rocks, floating debris and other obstructions. Port Deposit has a launch and fishing area on the south side of town.

Robert, Spencer, and Wood Islands near Port Deposit

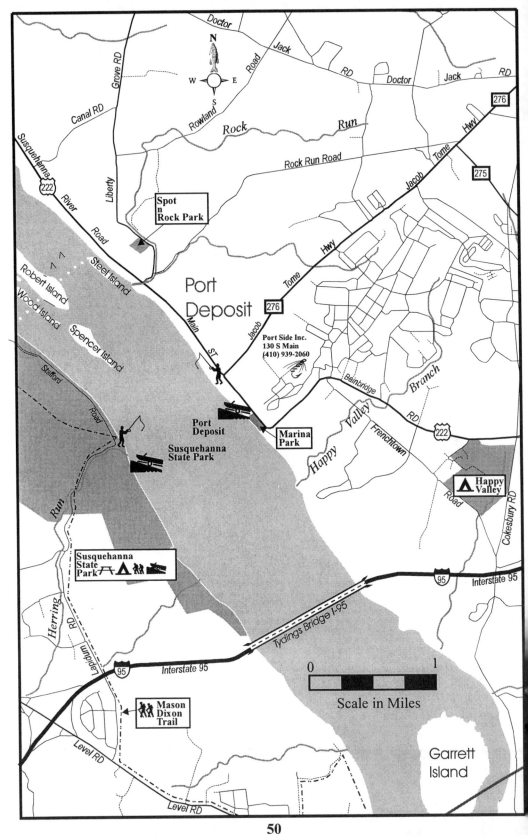

About a mile north of town, the boating ends (temporarily) as you hit Smith's Falls. It's not a waterfall really, but rather a shallow rocky region. Canoes, inflatables, and jonboats can still work this area, but it is tricky. Tides and fluctuations from the outlet of Conowingo Dam can result in rapidly changing water levels. This can leave you high and dry or put your landing site underwater very quickly. I have also fished in this area from a float tube, but I can't say that I recommend it. During the time I was in the water, a surge from Conowingo Dam raised the level and speed of the river to the point that I could not have gotten out where I put in. Luckily, I was putting my tube back in the car by then. Needless to say, be careful!

This area has large and smallmouth bass, stripers in season, sunfish, and white perch. Further up the west bank, Susquehanna State Park has excellent boating and fishing facilities as well as forests for hiking and birding.

Chapter Seven

Port Deposit to Conowingo

At nearly a mile long and a hundred feet high, the Conowingo Dam is the dominant structure in this section of the river. The word "Conowingo" comes from the Susquehannock tribe and meant "at the rapids." This hydroelectric facility was built in 1928 and is the first of several power generating facilities on the river. At peak operation, the dam produces about a half a megawatt of electricity. There is a fisherman's park with launch facilities, a catwalk on the face of the powerhouse, and bank fishing below the dam on the west bank. Catfish and stripers in Spring are the biggest attractions, but bass and panfish are also present. If the restoration is successful, the once famous shad fishery may also return. Extreme care must be taken when in the water downstream of the dam. Fluctuating power demands can result in rapid changes in the water volume coming out of the dam. Stay alert and be prepared to get out of the water if necessary. Tours of the hydroelectric facility and fish lifts are also available.

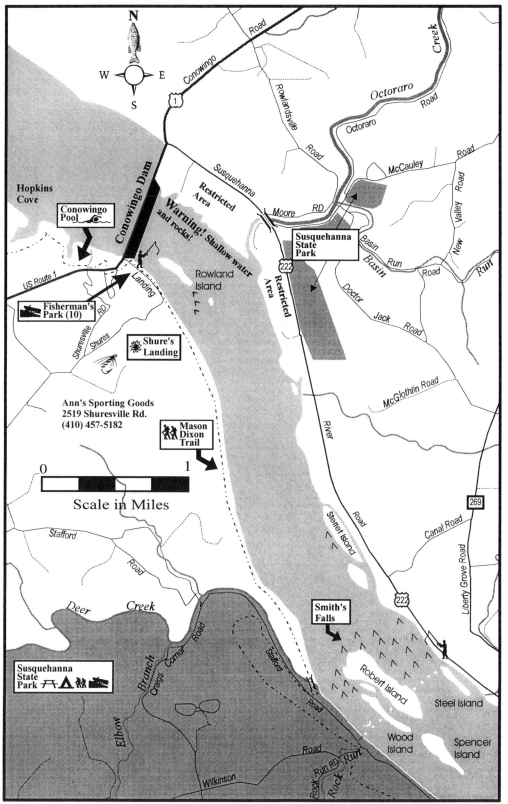

N
W E
S

Conowingo Road

① 1

Octoraro Creek

Rowlandsville Road

Octoraro Road

McCauley Road

New Valley Road

Hopkins Cove

Conowingo Pool

Conowingo Dam

Restricted Area

Susquehanna RD

Moore RD

Basin Run

Susquehanna State Park

② 222

Warning! Shallow water and rocks!

US Route 1

Landing

Rowland Island

Restricted Area

Doctor Jack Road

Fisherman's Park (10)

Shuresville RD

Shures RD

Shure's Landing

McGlothlin Road

Ann's Sporting Goods
2519 Shuresville Rd.
(410) 457-5182

Mason Dixon Trail

River Road

0 1

Scale in Miles

Stafford Road

Sterret Island

② 269

Canal Road

Liberty Grove Road

Deer Creek

Branch

Craigs Corner Road

Stafford Road

Smith's Falls

Robert Island

Steel Island

Susquehanna State Park

Elbow

Rock Run RD

Rock Run

Wood Island

Spencer Island

Wilkinson

Road

Tailrace area below Conowingo Dam

Other attractions include the Shures Landing Wildflower Area just below the dam on the west bank. This area is the premier parcel in a collection of wildflower sites in the lower Susquehanna Valley. This 1.75 mile long stretch of riparian floodplain was developed as a railroad spur during the construction of the dam. It was later abandoned after severe damage from hurricane Agnes. A wide variety of beautiful wildflowers and woodland trees grow along the old bed. Please leave them so that others may enjoy, too!

Chapter 8

Lake Conowingo

The floodwaters created by the Conowingo Dam create a 14 square mile reservoir suitable for boating and fishing. Numerous marinas and launches are available along its 35 miles of shoreline. This seventeen mile stretch of river extends up to just below the Holtwood dam near the town of the same name.

Shore access to the reservoir is somewhat limited due to steep terrain but boats provide many opportunities for birding and fishing. Although the reservoir spans the Pennsylvania/Maryland border, you may fish the entire lake with either type of fishing license. Try the coves and inlets of the lower portion of the impoundment for largemouth bass and panfish.

Conowingo Dam and Rowland Island

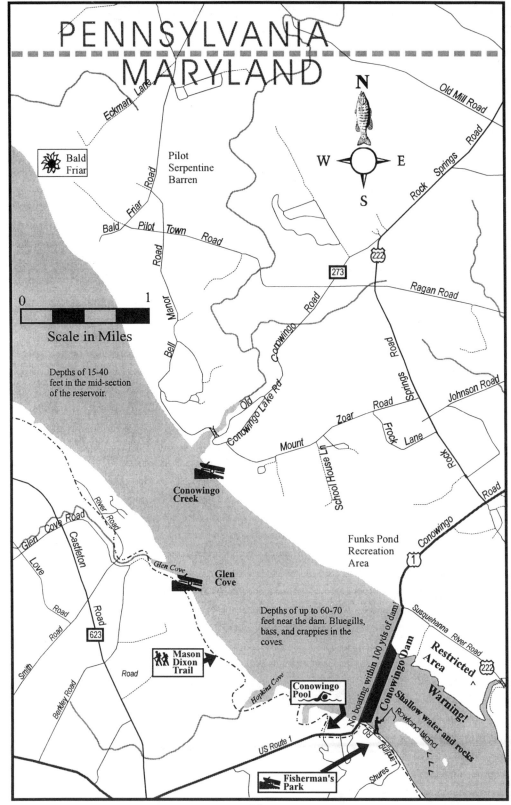

A bit more than half way up on the west bank is the Peach Bottom Atomic Power Station. Despite its cooling towers, there is still a warm water discharge from this plant. Striped bass, hybrids, and other fish congregate in this area during the cooler months. There is little or no bank access here, but launching a boat from the Peach Bottom access on the opposite bank can mean good fishing in the cooler months when the warm water is inviting. During the warm summer months, some of these same fish are found near the Muddy Run area.

Smallmouth are targeted in the upper portions of the reservoir amongst the rocky dropoff and slots near the islands. Other gamefish include walleye, muskies, catfish, and even some stocked trout.

Other activities in the area include a couple of relatively undeveloped wildflower areas on the east bank and good hiking on the Mason-Dixon trail near the lower west side. Birding is excellent with over 300 species found in the vicinity of the dam. A designated Bald Eagle Wintering Area is also found along the shore.

Peach Bottom Atomic Power Station

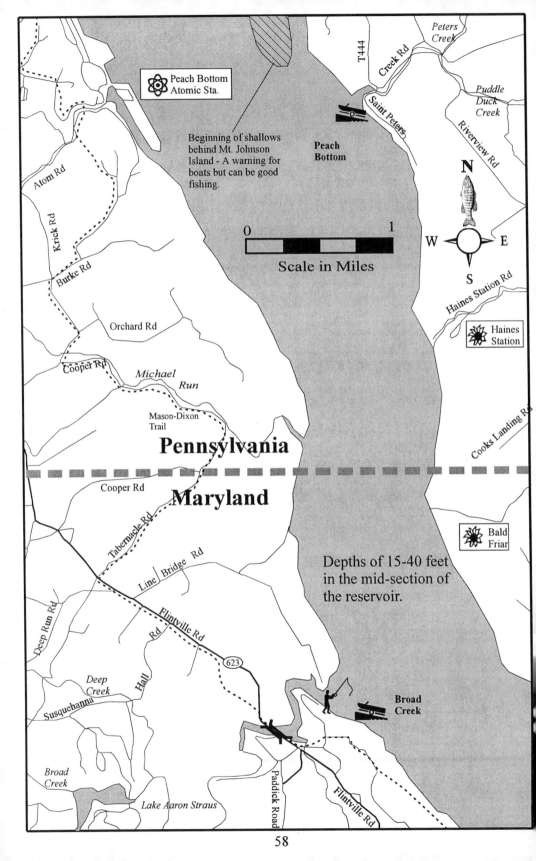

Peach Bottom
Atomic Sta.

Peters
Creek

Creek Rd

T444

Saint Peters

Puddle
Duck
Creek

Riverview Rd

Beginning of shallows
behind Mt. Johnson
Island - A warning for
boats but can be good
fishing.

Peach
Bottom

N

W   E

S

Atom Rd

Krick Rd

Burke Rd

0   1

Scale in Miles

Haines Station Rd

Orchard Rd

Haines
Station

Cooper Rd

Michael   Run

Mason-Dixon
Trail

Cooks Landing Rd

Pennsylvania

Cooper Rd

Maryland

Tabernacle Rd

Bald
Friar

Line Bridge Rd

Depths of 15-40 feet
in the mid-section of
the reservoir.

Deep Run Rd

Flintville Rd

Hall   Rd

623

Deep
Creek

Susquehanna

Broad
Creek

Broad
Creek

Paddick Road

Flintville Rd

Lake Aaron Straus

Chapter 9

Muddy Run to Holtwood Dam

Just below Holtwood is the Muddy Run pumped storage facility. This is basically a load-leveling device for electrical power demand. During times when excess power is generated, the pumps are run to fill the lake above. When the power is needed, it flows back down through turbine generators. There is a nice park surrounding this facility for picnicking, hiking, boating and fishing.

Just south of Muddy Run on the east bank is the Susquehannock State Park. While it is not a particularly large area, I found the woods there to be very pleasant and the view of the river spectacular.

Across from Muddy Run is the Bear Island area. This is an interesting stretch of river, particularly during times of low water. Always be aware, however, that the sound of sirens means water is being released from Holtwood and that you should evacuate the area immediately. As with most stretches of the river, I suggest wading with cleats to avoid slipping on the algae-coated ledgerock. A wading staff is also useful, regardless of your age. Ledgerock is present throughout much of the Susquehanna and provides excellent habitat for smallmouth and other gamefish. Typically, it is shaped a bit like a sawtooth. One side will be sloping while the other is abrupt. Keep this in mind while traversing the bottom.

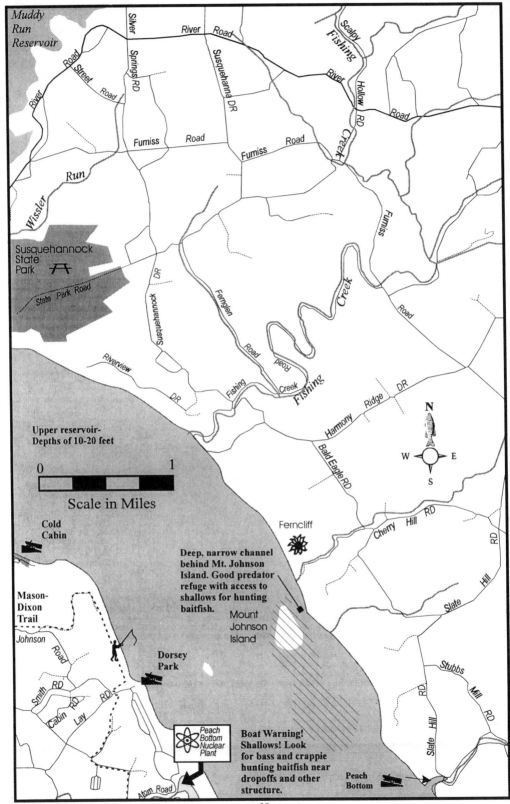

Muddy Run Reservoir

Silver Springs RD

River Road

Scalpy Fishing Creek

River Road Road Street

Road

Springs RD

Susquehanna DR

River

Hollow RD

Furniss Road

Furniss Road

Furniss Creek

Run

Wissler

Susquehannock State Park

State Park Road

Susquehannock DR

Fernglen Road Road

Fishing Creek

Road

Riverview DR

Fishing Creek

Fishing Creek

Harmony Ridge DR

Upper reservoir-
Depths of 10-20 feet

N

W E

S

Bald Eagle RD

0   1

Scale in Miles

Cold Cabin

Ferncliff

Cherry Hill RD

RD

Deep, narrow channel behind Mt. Johnson Island. Good predator refuge with access to shallows for hunting baitfish.

Slate Hill

Mason-Dixon Trail

Johnson Road

Mount Johnson Island

Smith RD

Cabin RD Lay RD

Dorsey Park

Peach Bottom Nuclear Plant

Slate Hill RD

Stubbs Mill RD

Boat Warning! Shallows! Look for bass and crappie hunting baitfish near dropoffs and other structure.

Peach Bottom

Atom Road

Once you are equipped for wading around the islands, you will be treated to interesting scenery, lots of wildlife, and good fishing. The islands and channels created by the river are fascinating and beautiful. The erosion of the rock and strength of the river during high water are clearly visible.

The Bear Island area is an excellent place for birding. There are colonies of gulls, many herons and egrets, soaring birds of prey, and woodland birds venturing out for insects. The activity level is high even during the middle of the day.

Muddy Run Reservoir above the Susquehanna

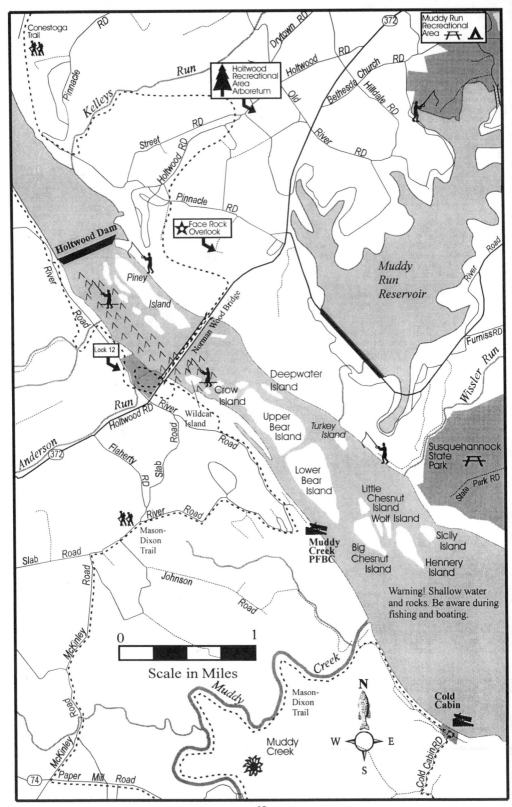

Muddy Run Recreational Area

Conestoga Trail

Kelleys Run

Pinnacle

Street RD

Holtwood RD

Holtwood Recreational Area Arboretum

Drytown RD

Holtwood RD

Old River RD

Bethesda Church RD

Hilldale RD

372

Pinnacle RD

Face Rock Overlook

Holtwood Dam

Piney Island

Norman Wood Bridge

Muddy Run Reservoir

River Road

Furniss RD

Wissler Run

River Road

Lock 12

Run

Holtwood RD

River Road

Anderson

372

Flaherty RD

Slab Road

Crow Island

Wildcat Island

River Road

Deepwater Island

Upper Bear Island

Turkey Island

Lower Bear Island

Susquehannock State Park

State Park RD

Muddy Creek PFBC

Little Chesnut Island

Wolf Island

Big Chesnut Island

Sicily Island

Hennery Island

Slab Road

River Road

Mason-Dixon Trail

Johnson Road

Warning! Shallow water and rocks. Be aware during fishing and boating.

McKinley Road

0   1

Scale in Miles

Muddy

Creek

Mason-Dixon Trail

N

W   E

S

Cold Cabin

McKinley Road

74

Paper Mill Road

Muddy Creek

Cold Cabin RD

Since this is an area you want to visit during low water conditions, the river will be dropping or low and steady. During this time, fish move out of the smaller side channels into the central portions of the river to avoid being trapped in a pool that may run dry. You will, in fact, find minnows in these tenuous spots. The larger fish that you're after will tend to be in the central stream of the river toward the east bank. However, the hiking is more interesting coming from the west. Once you get to the river, two tactics will help you find fish. In the swift center currents, use jigs or heavily weighted flies to get down to where the fish are sheltered from the current. Be prepared to lose some tackle in the rocks! The other technique is to work the eddies of the main current. In this area, poppers and shallow diving plugs or flies are more appropriate. Imitations of crayfish and minnows are good bets. Look for naturals in the shallow pools near the edge of the river. If you can't find any, try chartreuse/white Deep Minnows and ruddy brown crayfish flies or lures.

Surprisingly, power boats can access the main channel in this area even during low water. Shallow draft boats such as canoes or inflatables can access even more area.

Chapter 10

Lake Aldred

The 2400 acre impoundment created above Holtwood Dam is surrounded by an excellent set of hiking trails ranging from an easy half hour jaunt to the cross-country Mason-Dixon Trail. Holtwood Dam is also the lower limit of the Pennsylvania Fish and Boat Commission's Big Bass Program. The special rules enacted created a minimum size limit of 15" on all bass caught in the Susquehanna between Holtwood Dam and the Fabridam in Sunbury.

Holtwood powerhouse

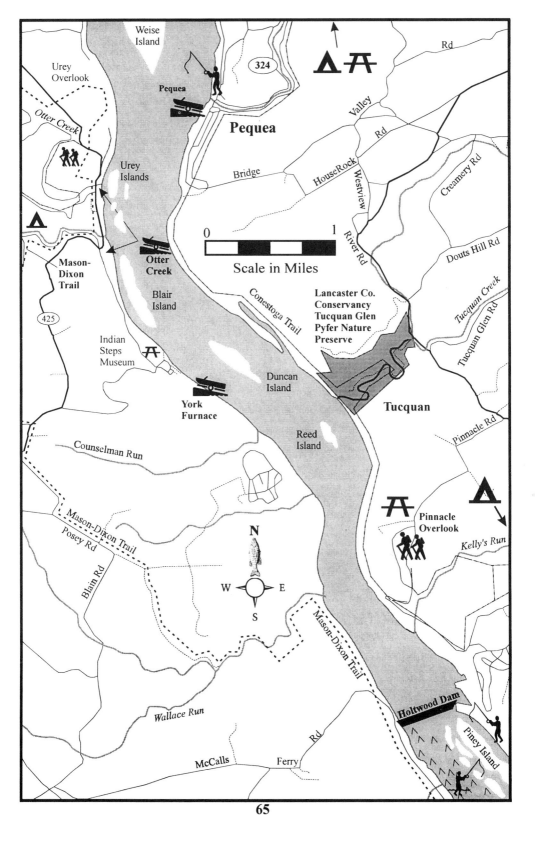

Weise
Island

Urey
Overlook

324

Pequea

Rd

Pequea

Otter Creek

Valley

Rd

HouseRock

Westview

Creamery Rd

Urey
Islands

Bridge

River Rd

Douts Hill Rd

Mason-
Dixon
Trail

425

Otter
Creek

Blair
Island

0   1

Scale in Miles

Tucquan Creek

Lancaster Co.
Conservancy
Tucquan Glen
Pyfer Nature
Preserve

Tucquan Glen Rd

Indian
Steps
Museum

Conestoga Trail

Duncan
Island

York
Furnace

Tucquan

Counselman Run

Reed
Island

Pinnacle Rd

Mason-Dixon Trail

Posey Rd

N

Pinnacle
Overlook

Blain Rd

W   E

Kelly's Run

S

Mason-Dixon Trail

Wallace Run

Rd

Holtwood Dam

McCalls   Ferry

Piney Island

Improved fishing is already apparent in this stretch of the river. If you do catch a fish above the limit, it's best to return it to the water anyway since it took six or more years for the fish to reach that impressive size and weight.

Once you are mid-way up Lake Aldred, there are boat ramps available on both sides of the river.

Just below Safe Harbor Dam is the tailrace area. There are several attractions here. Good fishing can often be found for smallmouth and other species. The Shenk's Ferry Wildflower Area is particularly lovely in the spring when the first blooms are arriving. Many maps show a Shenk's Ferry on both sides of the river, so it's important to remember that the Wildflower Refuge is on the east bank. There is also lots of room for picnicking and a nice overlook of the river where you can see four miles downstream and three miles upstream. The arboretum in Safe Harbor Park has some trails and over fifty species of trees.

Safe Harbor Dam Tailrace

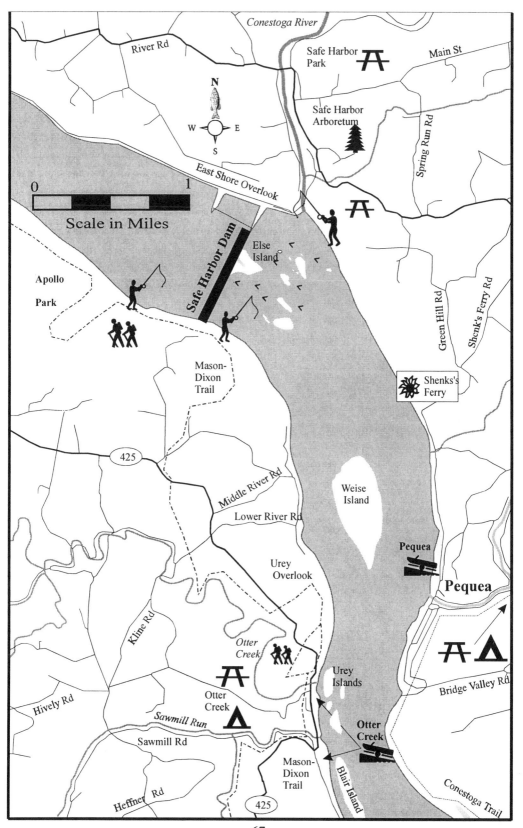

Chapter 11

Lake Clarke

The Safe Harbor Dam was created in 1931 and creates a 5000 acre reservoir named Lake Clarke. It's roughly a dozen miles long and backs water up to the town of Columbia. The Safe Harbor area offers fishing, a river overlook, an arboretum, picnicking, and boat launching facilities.

This area can be used for power boating, but beware of rocks, especially during low water and near islands. Largemouth and smallmouth bass, panfish, walleye, and catfish are common in this area.

Birding is popular on Rookery Island, but remember that it is closed to access from March 1 to July 31 to protect nesting birds. A small boat is a great way view the nesters from a safe distance during this time.

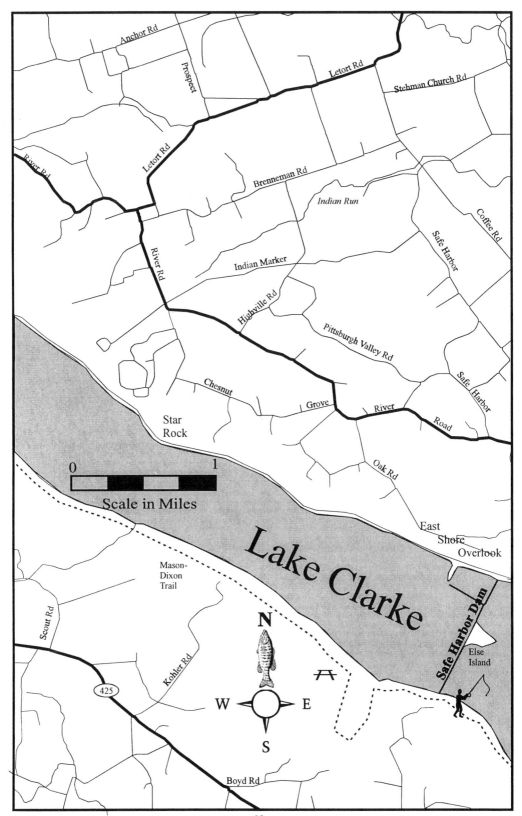

Chapter 12

Columbia to York Haven

One of the unique attractions of this stretch of river is Chickie's Rock State Park, just north of Columbia on the east side of the river.

Not only does the park have hiking, picnicking, and a beautiful overlook of the river, it also has one of the few established rock-climbing areas in eastern Pennsylvania.

Rock-climbing does have its inherent dangers and you should always learn from a qualified instructor before taking to the rock. Chickie's is a good place to learn because there is a reasonable range of difficulty and most areas can be top-roped. This means that you can walk behind the rock and establish an anchor near the top before you start climbing. This allows the climbers to alternate ascents while the other provides tension on the rope to prevent a fall. This area can get crowded, especially on weekends, so always wear a helmet to protect yourself from rocks jarred loose by other climbers. Below you can see the main face of Chickie's Rock.

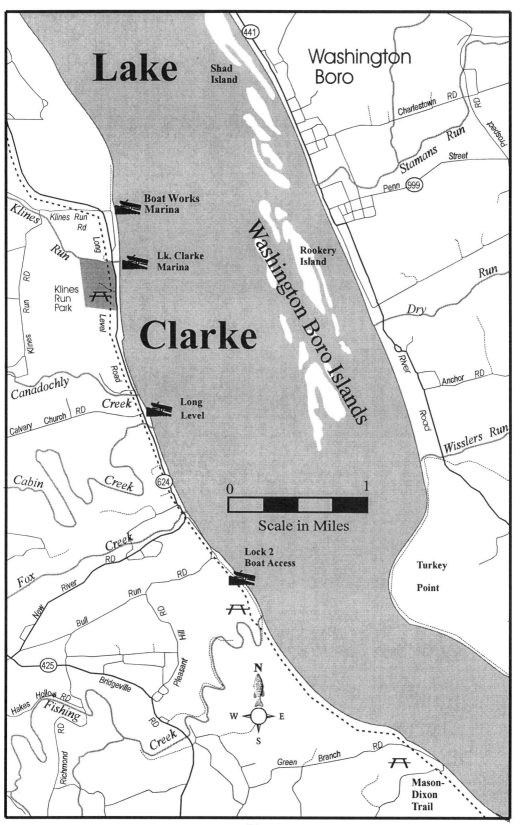

Lake

Shad
Island

Washington
Boro

441

Charlestown RD RD

Prospect

Stamans Run

Street

Penn 999

Boat Works
Marina

Klines
Run
Rd

Klines

Run

RD

Long

Level

Rookery
Island

Lk. Clarke
Marina

Dry Run

Klines
Run
Park

River Road

Anchor RD

Klines

Canadochly

Creek

Road

Clarke

Washington Boro Islands

Long
Level

Calvary Church RD

Wisslers Run

Cabin

Creek

Creek

624

0   1

Scale in Miles

Fox

Creek

RD

Turkey

Point

River

RD

Run RD

Lock 2
Boat Access

New

Bull

Hill

Pleasant

425

N

Bridgeville

Hakes Hollow RD

Fishing

RD

RD

W   E

S

Richmond

Creek

Green   Branch   RD

Mason-
Dixon
Trail

Chickie's Rock

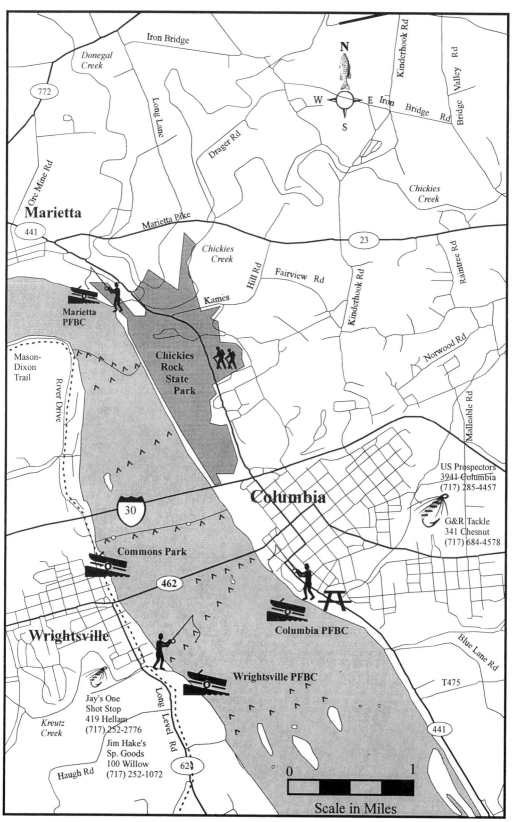

Iron Bridge

Donegal
Creek

772

Long Lane

Drager Rd

Chickies
Creek

N

W ⊕ E Iron Bridge Rd

S

Kinderhook Rd

Valley Rd

Bridge

Ore Mine Rd

Marietta

441

Marietta Pike

23

Chickies
Creek

Chickies
Creek

Hill Rd

Fairview Rd

Kinderhook Rd

Raintree Rd

Kames

**Marietta
PFBC**

Mason-
Dixon
Trail

River Drive

**Chickies
Rock
State
Park**

Norwood Rd

Malleable Rd

30

Columbia

**US Prospectors
3941 Columbia
(717) 285-4457**

**G&R Tackle
341 Chesnut
(717) 684-4578**

Commons Park

462

Columbia PFBC

Wrightsville

Wrightsville PFBC

Blue Lane Rd

T475

Long Level Rd

Jay's One
Shot Stop
419 Hellam
(717) 252-2776

Kreutz
Creek

Jim Hake's
Sp. Goods
100 Willow
(717) 252-1072

Haugh Rd

624

441

0   1

Scale in Miles

Technical climbs are rated in difficulty from 5.0 to 5.13. Originally, the scale only went to 5.10, which was deemed impossible. Then somebody did it! The "impossible" routes were then called 5.11. Climbers and climbing gear improved and these routes fell, too. Today, no route is considered truly impossible since modern tools can allow skilled climbers to ascend a vertical, featureless, face by drilling holes in the rock and placing protective anchors. Many climbers view this as "cheating" and eschew this practice. Modern climbing ethics emphasize minimizing damage to rock. This means not only avoiding bolts and pitons, but using natural colored chalk to avoid leaving a lot of white marks on popular routes. The chalk is for getting a good grip with the sweaty palms that climbing exposure induces!

I have visited this area several times and climbed the front face. The route I normally chose would rank about a 5.7 or 5.8 based on other areas I have been to. None of the routes is tougher than about 5.9. There are also smaller cliffs and boulders nearby for learning the techniques. This practice, often called bouldering, is a good way to build confidence and allow an instructor to physically help you with hand and foot placement, body position and balance, and proper use of equipment.

This portion of the river also has some great fishing. The rocky areas near Columbia provide lots of cover and good smallmouth fishing. Further upstream you will find the mouth of Codorus Creek and the Haldemann Riffle. This is my favorite place to fish in the entire river. At stages below four feet, the wading is good and there is an excellent variety of lies and cover for fish. I have caught smallmouth, walleye, channel catfish, and bluegills here. The water in this area is still affected by the Brunner Island power plant, so it can be a bit too warm in the summer.

As you move up toward the plant, you will pass through the small town of Saginaw on the west bank. I have also had good luck here, particularly when the water is up slightly and the fish are in the eddies and cover close to the bank.

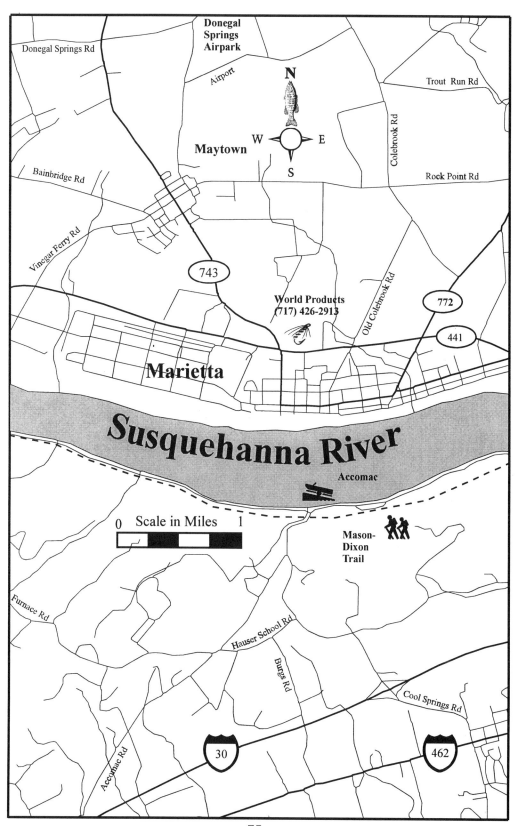

Donegal
Springs
Airpark

Donegal Springs Rd

Airport

Trout Run Rd

N

Maytown

W   E

S

Colebrook Rd

Bainbridge Rd

Rock Point Rd

Vinegar Ferry Rd

743

World Products
(717) 426-2913

Old Colebrook Rd

772

441

Marietta

Susquehanna River

Accomac

Scale in Miles
0   1

Mason-
Dixon
Trail

Furnace Rd

Hauser School Rd

Burgs Rd

Cool Springs Rd

Accomac Rd

30

462

The area near the Brunner Island plant can be excellent if the natural water temperature is cold. At these times, the warm discharge from the coal-burning plant draws fish. It also draws fishermen! I can remember cold November days where it actually felt good to stick your hand in the water since it was markedly warmer than the air. As odd as it sounds, there are times it produces good fishing. I have caught smallmouth, walleye, and channel cats in this area. During the summer, the area near the plant will have fewer fish if the plant is in operation since the water can rise to more than 100°F. At this temperature, the water can't carry enough oxygen to support most fish.

Brunner Island power plant

At the upper end of this stretch is the York Haven Dam. It is a power generating dam built in 1901 and producing power since 1904. There are twenty turbines which can produce about 20,000 kilowatts. The dam is currently being upgraded with a shad lift that is planned for completion in the spring of 2000. It will be the last large major retrofit in the shad restoration plan. Hopefully, a strong shad run can be rebuilt throughout much of the watershed. For now, fishermen come looking for walleye, smallmouth, and muskellunge in the tailrace area. The shallow areas near the spillway portions of the dam are also worth investigating.

York Haven Dam

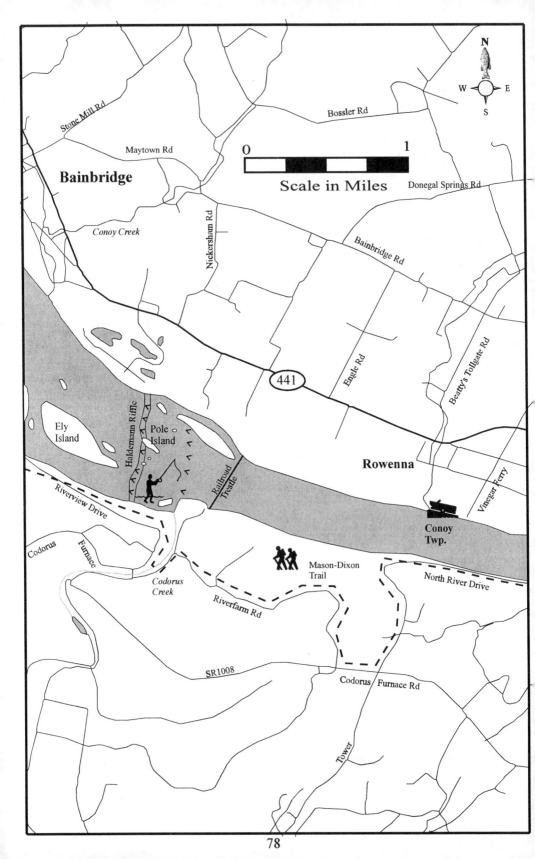

Chapter 13

York Haven to Harrisburg

Certainly the most famous feature in this portion of the river is Three Mile Island (TMI). The reason for its fame depends upon who you ask. Most folks that do not live near the river remember TMI primarily for its nuclear reactor. Those living nearby are more likely to think about premier smallmouth habitat than anything else. Even so, they DO remember the accident.

On March 28, 1979, TMI #2 was operating at near full capacity when a pump failed causing the reactor to shut itself down. The intense heat from the fissioning core caused a relief valve to open and allow radioactive water to enter the containment building. So far, this was within the design of the system. Unfortunately, the relief valve stuck open even after conditions had changed such that it should have closed. For nearly two hours the cooling water leaked out undetected.

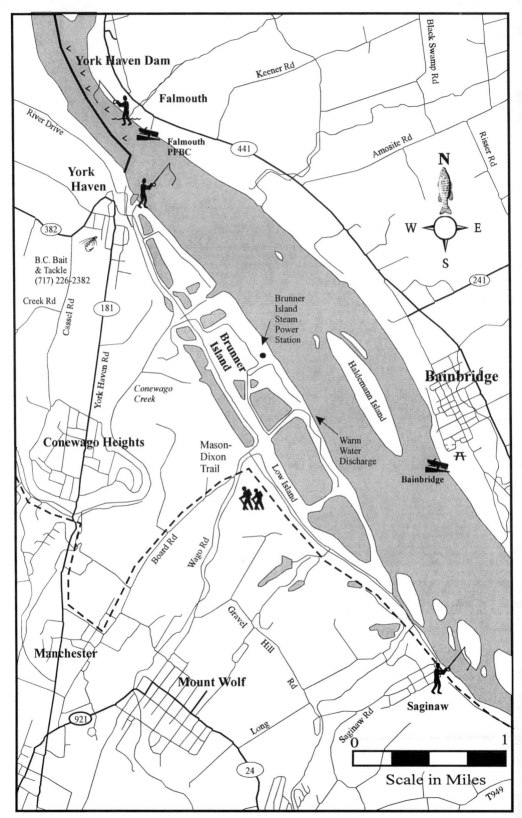

York Haven Dam

Falmouth

Keener Rd

Black Swamp Rd

River Drive

Falmouth PFBC

441

Amosite Rd

Risser Rd

York Haven

N

W   E

S

382

B.C. Bait & Tackle
(717) 226-2382

241

Creek Rd

Cassel Rd

181

Brunner
Island
Steam
Power
Station

Bainbridge

York Haven Rd

Brunner Island

Conewago Creek

Haldemann Island

Conewago Heights

Mason-Dixon Trail

Warm Water Discharge

Bainbridge

Board Rd

Wago Rd

Low Island

Manchester

Gravel Hill Rd

Mount Wolf

921

Long

24

Saginaw Rd

Saginaw

0   1

Scale in Miles

T949

Eventually, this uncovered the hot core of the reactor and some of the uranium core melted. Finally, the valve was discovered and water was supplied into the core once again. The mixture of the cool water and hot core caused some further damage to the uranium rods. A catastrophe was averted, but not by a large margin. A huge cleanup was undertaken and nearly a million gallons of contaminated water was removed from the containment building. The water was evaporated in such a fashion to retain the radioactive components. Most of the residual radioactive materials from TMI #2 were shipped to a site in Idaho. The entire event points out two very important points about nuclear energy:

1) Humans and human designed systems are imperfect. Despite a commendable uptime record, the downside risk of a cataclysmic meltdown in these reactors is pretty frightening.

2) Even without the accident, a certain amount of radioactive waste is generated that we don't know what to do with. Right now, we send it to Idaho or Nevada and hope it doesn't escape into the environment and hurt any living thing.

All forms of power generation have their costs and dangers. We must face them objectively and choose the balance of solutions that can meet our needs in the most sustainable, environmentally sound fashion.

Okay, back to Three Mile Island. The area around TMI is heavily monitored and the air, water, and wildlife have a clean bill of health. The smallmouth fishing in the area can be excellent and a lot of boats launch from the Goldsboro and Middletown ramps. There is excellent habitat through much of this stretch and wadable areas near Middletown and New Cumberland during low water. The lake-like region in the Goldsboro area (due to York Haven Dam) is actually called Lake Frederic. In addition to smallmouth, there are also largemouth, panfish, walleye, muskies, and catfish. Several of the islands have excellent picnic areas.

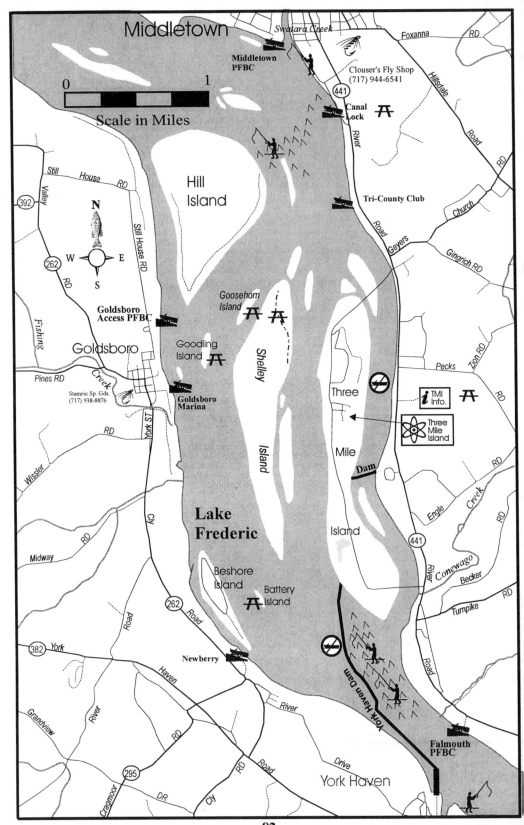

Middletown

Swatara Creek

Middletown
PFBC

Clouser's Fly Shop
(717) 944-6541

441

Canal
Lock

Foxanna   RD

Hillsdale   Road

0   1
Scale in Miles

Hill
Island

Tri-County Club

Church   RD

Geyers   Road   River

Gingrich RD

Still   House   RD

392

Still House RD

N
W   E
S

262   RD

Fishing

Goldsboro
Access PFBC

Goosehorn
Island

Goldsboro

Goodling
Island

Shelley

Pecks   Road

Zion RD

Pines RD

Stamric Sp. Gds.
(717) 938-8876

Creek

Goldsboro
Marina

Three

TMI
Info.

Three
Mile
Island

York ST

Island   Mile

Dam

RD

Wissler   RD

Cly

Lake
Frederic

Island

441

River   Conewago

Engle   Creek   RD

Midway   RD

Becker

Beshore
Island

Battery
Island

Turnpike   RD

262   Road

382   York

Newberry

York Haven Dam

Road

Road

River

Haven   RD   River

GrandView

295

Cragmoor   DR

Cly   RD   Road

Drive

Falmouth
PFBC

York Haven

Three Mile Island Nuclear Power Station

Moving upstream into Harrisburg is a study in contrasts. You will first pass Highspire and Steelton. While the fishing can be excellent here, much of the eastern shore is less than picturesque. Decaying steel mills and other industries create a harsh backdrop for the gently flowing river.

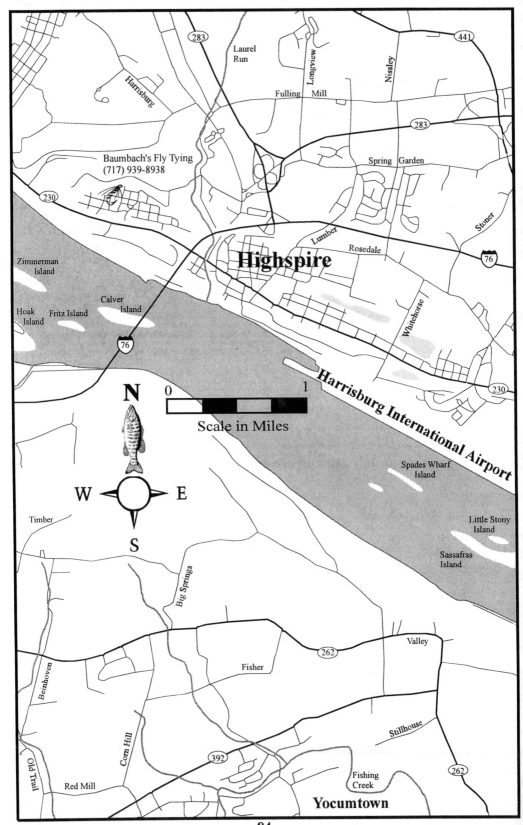

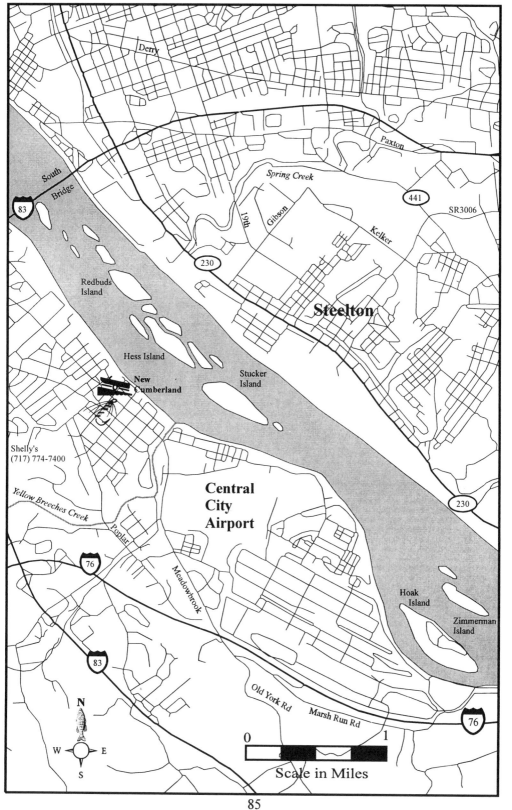

Derry

South
Bridge

83

Spring Creek

441

SR3006

19th

Gibson

Kelker

230

Redbuds
Island

Steelton

Hess Island

New
Cumberland

Stucker
Island

Shelly's
(717) 774-7400

Yellow Breeches Creek

Poplar

230

**Central
City
Airport**

76

Meadowbrook

Hoak
Island

Zimmerman
Island

83

N

W — E

S

Old York Rd

Marsh Run Rd

76

0   1

Scale in Miles

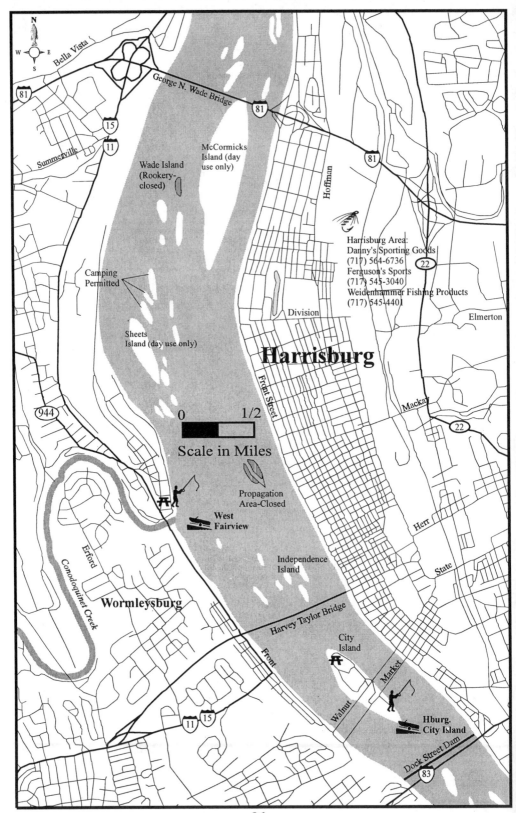

Central Harrisburg and City Island

In central Harrisburg, on the other hand, the river corridor is blessed with a green belt on the east bank that is used by many city residents. Bikers, strollers, and fishermen are visible against a well kept strip of green. In this stretch, the city has done a better job of making the mighty river a positive feature in its landscape.

City Island in central Harrisburg is probably the most civilized island in the Susquehanna. You can take in a baseball game, ride the railroad, eat, swim, fish, and stroll. It is intended for day use only, but a full day of activities is quite possible. The island is also the terminus of the new Susquehanna River Trail. A log jam and the Dock Street Dam pose serious impediments just downstream of City Island.

Chapter 14

Harrisburg to Fort Hunter

The next area described in this guide extends from downtown Harrisburg to the area near Marysville. The Sheets Island Archipelago on the north edge of Harrisburg provides excellent fishing and exploring opportunities. Sheets island itself is intended for day use only, but surrounding islands may have camping spots at low water levels. Despite the remains of an early homestead on the north end of the island, Sheets has some prime bottomland hardwood forest. The large island upstream from Sheets is McCormick. This island is owned by the City of Harrisburg and has good picnic spots on the south end. The small island adjacent to McCormick is Wade island. This area is closed because it is a rookery for Great Egrets and Black-Crowned Night Herons. Bring the binoculars along and take a look from your canoe.

At Rockville, a railroad bridge crosses the river. It is 3,280 feet long and is the longest stone-arch bridge in the world. It opened in 1902 and still carries many trains a day.

Marysville is directly across the river from Fort Hunter. There are ramps on both sides of the river. At low water levels typical during the summer months, both sides of the river have access to easily wadable areas. My experience in this area occurred before the "Big Bass" regulations were extended to include this stretch as is the case now. Back then, we would spend the evening wading and casting among the small islands as the sun set. We always caught good numbers of fish, although most were small. Hopefully, the average size is now on the rise as has happened in other areas that have the more protective regulation.

Family outings can be based from Fort Hunter since it has a variety of attractions. Besides fishing, there is a nice 37 acre park for picnicking and the historic Fort Hunter mansion. Another fun feature for nature lovers is that many of the trees near the mansion have placards which identify them. This is educational for kids and adults. There are some very familiar trees as well as some imported species.

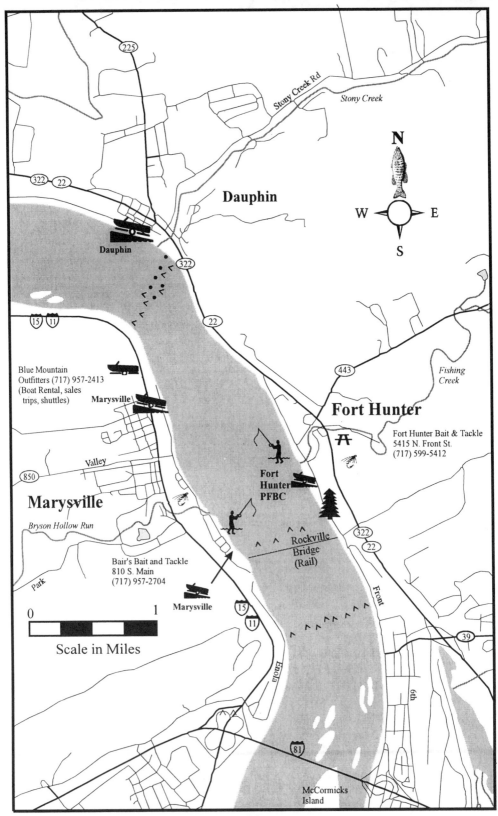

Stony Creek Rd   Stony Creek

N

Dauphin

W ● E

S

225

322 22

Dauphin

322

22

15 11

Blue Mountain
Outfitters (717) 957-2413
(Boat Rental, sales
trips, shuttles)

443   Fishing
                        Creek

Marysville

Fort Hunter

Valley

Fort Hunter Bait & Tackle
5415 N. Front St.
(717) 599-5412

850

Marysville

Fort
Hunter
PFBC

Bryson Hollow Run

Rockville
Bridge
(Rail)

322

22

Bair's Bait and Tackle
810 S. Main
(717) 957-2704

Front

Park

Marysville

15

11

Enola

39

0   1

Scale in Miles

6th

81

McCormicks
Island

Chapter 15

Fort Hunter to Halifax

Just above Fort Hunter the river narrows at Dauphin. Here the river has eroded a cut through the Appalachian Mountains. This ridge is called Second Mountain on the east side and Cove Mountain on the west. Several more ridges are traversed between here and Duncannon. Good smallmouth fishing can often be found in the riffles and pockets in this area. Some parts are wadable at low water, but this also means that boating is a bit tricky. To pass through without scraping or bumping, try the far left channel.

Dauphin Narrows

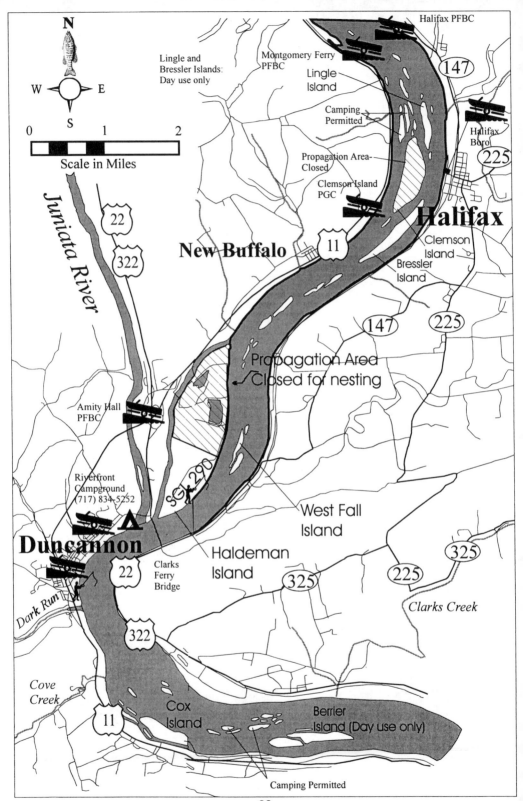

Moving upstream you'll find another spot where the river is crowded in on each side. Peters Mountain is the name of the ridge just before Duncannon. The river is not the only thing crowded here. The roads running on each side of the river, highways 11/15 and 22/322 are narrow, winding, and often crowded. Be careful and have a safe outing!

The Appalachian National Scenic Trail crosses the river at Duncannon, but only follows it for a few miles.

The Juniata River flows into the Susquehanna just above Duncannon. The Juniata is the second largest tributary constituting about one eighth of the total watershed. The river is roughly 100 miles long and has many recreational opportunities of its own. I have not fished in the Juniata, but am told that the lower river has some excellent smallmouth areas. The upper tributaries are cool enough to support trout populations. The Van Dyke Research Station is also on the river — it is the shad hatchery that is helping to restore the shad run to the Susquehanna.

Right near the mouth of the Juniata is Haldeman Island. This is State Game Land, but walk-in access is closed to protect waterfowl nesting on the north end of the island. The south end of the island is accessible by boat and hiking and birding are possibilities on the southern tip. The Halifax area has boat ramps and some wadable fishing areas. There is also a small park in town.

Chapter 16

Halifax to Selinsgrove

Just above Halifax on the east bank is the Halifax access. This is the start of the Susquehanna River Trail. Although many parts of the river are suitable for river trips, the Pennsylvania Fish and Boat Commission is working with the Alliance for the Chesapeake Bay to make the stretch from Millersburg to Harrisburg especially "user-friendly." Public access points are labeled as "trailheads" and certain islands are marked as suitable for overnight camping. This is a new effort and more information is becoming available. This area and the portion of the river above are excellent for canoe trips. There are many islands to explore and camp on plus good fishing and sightseeing along the way.

River access can be obtained at Montgomery Ferry on the west bank of the river, but there is a catch — you can only get there by driving northbound on highway 11/15. The road is divided and there is no break in the divider at smaller structures such as boat ramps. I suspect this done for safety reasons and is repeated at several of the ramps in this section of the river where the busy highway runs close to the river. So, if you are southbound, you'll have to overshoot a bit and double back.

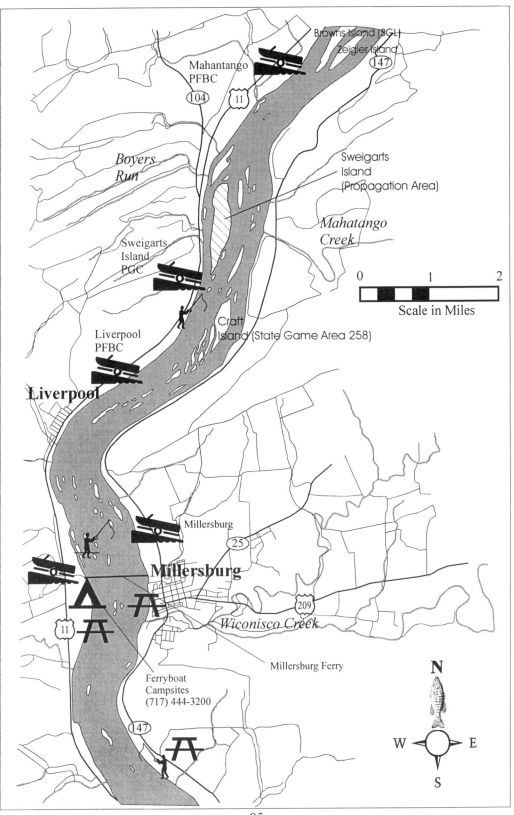

Browns Island (SGL)
Zeigler Island
(147)

Mahantango
PFBC
(104)
(11)

*Boyers
Run*

Sweigarts
Island
(Propagation Area)

*Mahatango
Creek*

Sweigarts
Island
PGC

0   1   2

Scale in Miles

Craft
Island (State Game Area 258)

Liverpool
PFBC

Liverpool

Millersburg
(25)

Millersburg

(209)

(11)

Wiconisco Creek

Millersburg Ferry

Ferryboat
Campsites
(717) 444-3200

(147)

N

W ⊙ E

S

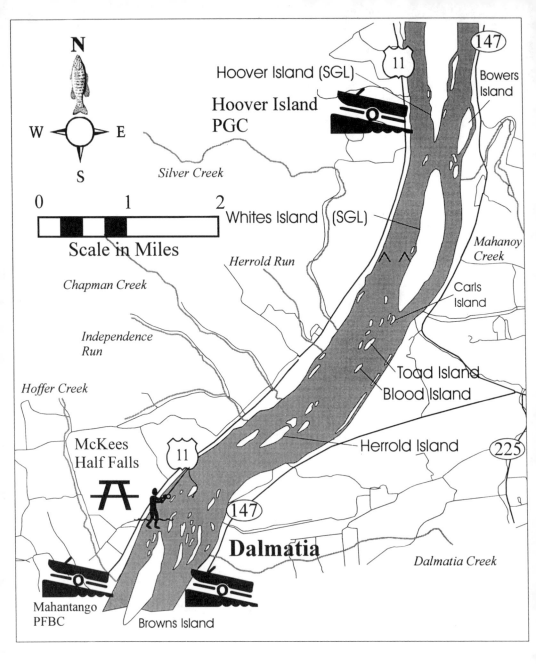

N

W E

S

0 1 2

Scale in Miles

Silver Creek

Chapman Creek

Independence
Run

Hoffer Creek

Herrold Run

Hoover Island (SGL)

Hoover Island
PGC

Whites Island (SGL)

Bowers
Island

147

11

Mahanoy
Creek

Carls
Island

Toad Island

Blood Island

Herrold Island

225

McKees
Half Falls

11

147

Dalmatia

Dalmatia Creek

Mahantango
PFBC

Browns Island

Once you get into the northbound lanes, there are numerous public and private ramps along this stretch of river. The town of Millersburg also has a ferry. It was the first commercial ferry to cross the Susquehanna starting in 1825 and runs for about a mile across the river. Several other ferries have also operated on the river, but as bridges were built, most have gone out of business. The Millersburg ferry is now the only one still in operation.

Just above the P.F.B.C. access at Mahantango, there is a small park called the Snyder County Rest Area. It is actually near a double rock line crossing the river know as McKees Half Falls. This is a very accessible area that has some interesting fishing opportunities. At low water, you can wade near the rocks and catch smallmouth bass and panfish. Other fish may be available, but that's what I've found!

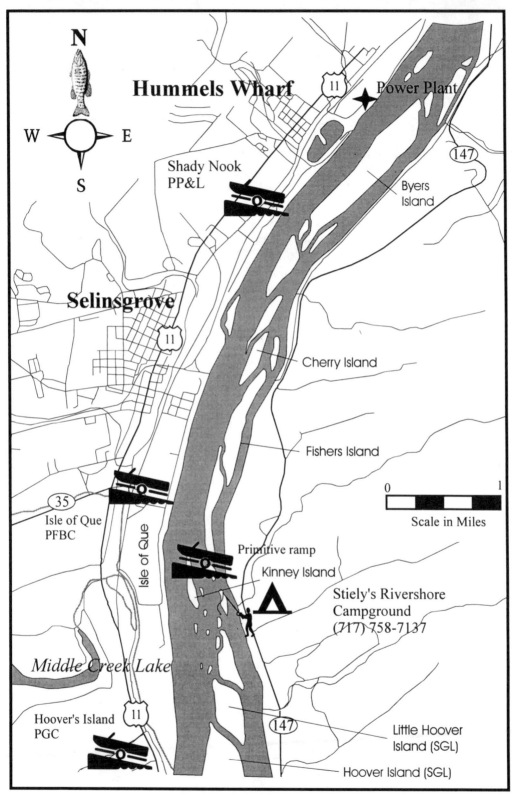

Chapter 17

Selinsgrove to Sunbury

This stretch of river has a truly unique feature — the longest inflatable dam in the world is located on the Susquehanna just below Sunbury. Dubbed the "Fabridam," it consists of seven inflatable rubber bags eight feet in diameter. The bags are each about 300 feet long except the seventh which completes the span and is 175 feet. The bags are anchored to concrete pilings and create a total length that exceeds 2,000 feet. The dam was desired for recreation such as sailing and power boating, but a conventional dam was avoided due to flooding concerns. Construction began in 1966 and initial opening was slated for July 4, 1969 after delays due to river fluctuations. As the final bag was inflated, it burst. This would not be the last time. Difficulties with the bags continued for nearly fifteen years until a new supplier was able to make a more reliable bag and attachment system.

Fabridam fishing

The dam is now typically inflated in the summer months to create "Lake Augusta," the temporary impoundment which adds two to three feet of water depth. Deeper draft boats are then viable from the dam up to the confluence area and Shikellamy State Park on Packers Island. The park actually has two parts. The first is on the island and consists of a marina plus areas for hiking, fishing, bicycling, and picnicking. On the west side of the confluence there is also a high bluff that is part of the park. Although this area is small, the view is spectacular. My only sadness on viewing this panorama was the clearly visible difference in the water clarity between the two branches of the river. Although both parts of the watershed have suffered from coal mining, industry, and poor agricultural practices, the lower West Branch looks clear from up on the bluff. Even during dry summer weather, the North Branch or main stream of the Susquehanna is visibly murky.

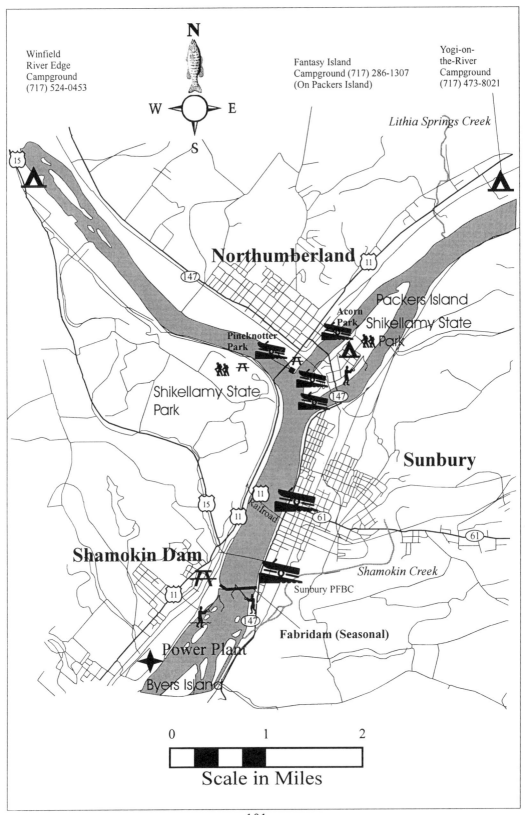

I could not help but think back to earlier that day when I had come down from Wilkes-Barre and witnessed the disgusting orange color of several tributaries destroyed by the effluents of mines. It has been many years since most of the mines closed and it will be even more before the streams run clean again unless we devote the time and money to enable the healing.

The "Forks" where the West and North Branches meet

Chapter 18

Sunbury to Wilkes-Barre

From Sunbury upstream, the main portion of the river is either called the North Branch of the Susquehanna or just the Susquehanna, depending on which map you look at. As near as I can tell, it is a common name used primarily by some Pennsylvanians in this region.

In any case, this branch of the river extends well past the Pennsylvania border to Otsego Lake near Cooperstown, New York. The Pennsylvania portion of the river has suffered due to coal mine effluents from the rich deposits near the river and its tributaries. It's interesting to note that the reduced water quality has not affected all fish equally. Resident fish may not fare quite as well, but biologists say that shad fry planted here actually fare somewhat better than in the West Branch. Maybe it's because they spend most of their life at sea!

The Susquehanna Riverlands Park above Berwick provides a nice place for picnics and short hikes, provided you don't mind being in the shadow of a nuclear energy station's cooling tower.

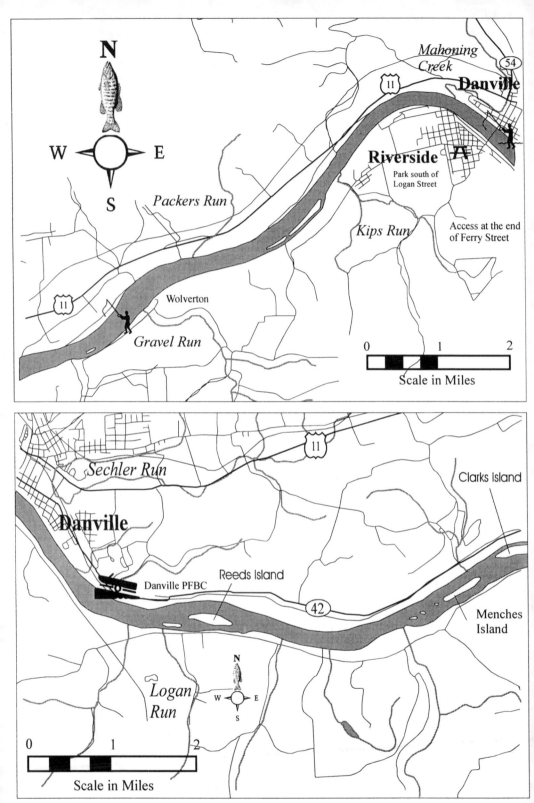

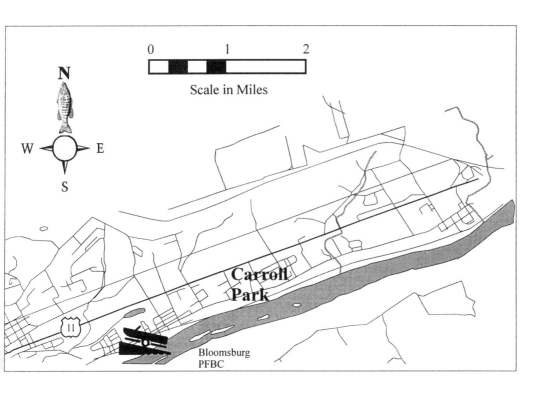

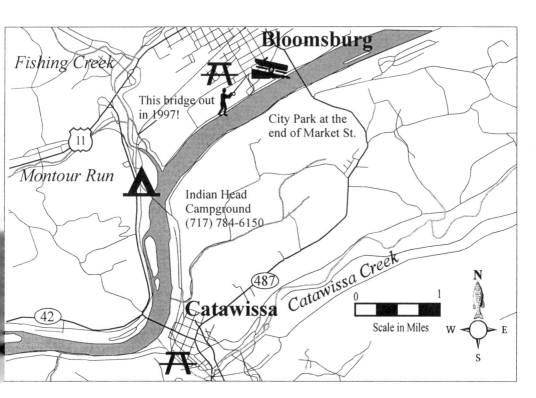

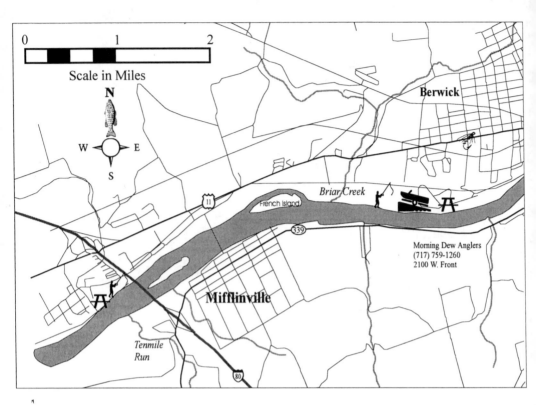

Scale in Miles

N

W ⬦ E

S

French Island

Briar Creek

Berwick

11

339

Mifflinville

Tenmile
Run

80

Morning Dew Anglers
(717) 759-1260
2100 W. Front

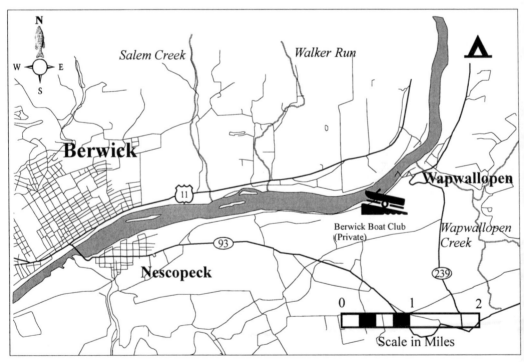

N

W ⬦ E

S

Salem Creek

Walker Run

Berwick

11

Nescopeck

93

Berwick Boat Club
(Private)

Wapwallopen

Wapwallopen
Creek

239

0   1   2

Scale in Miles

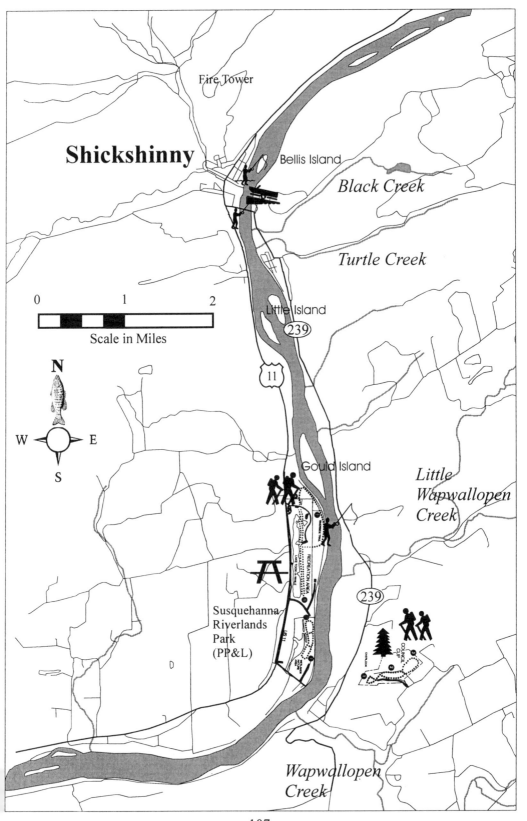

Fire Tower

Shickshinny

Bellis Island

Black Creek

Turtle Creek

Little Island

239

11

0   1   2
Scale in Miles

N
W E
S

Gould Island

Little Wapwallopen Creek

239

Susquehanna
Riverlands
Park
(PP&L)

COUNCIL CUP

Wapwallopen Creek

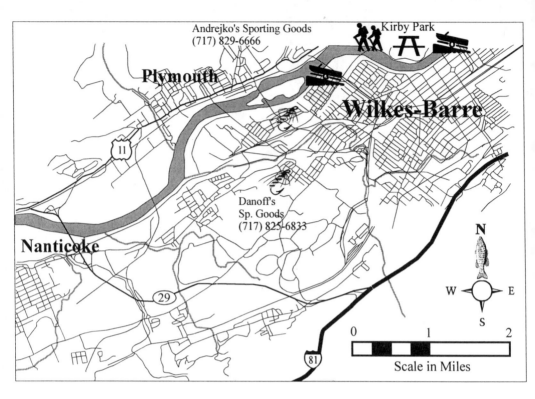

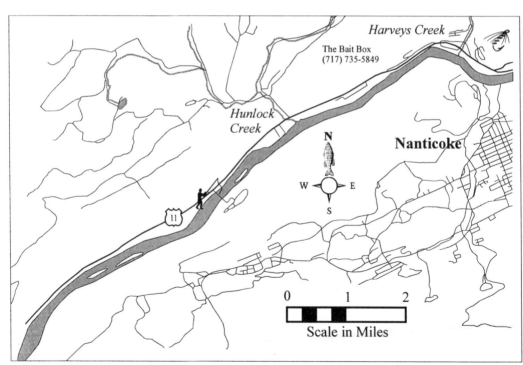

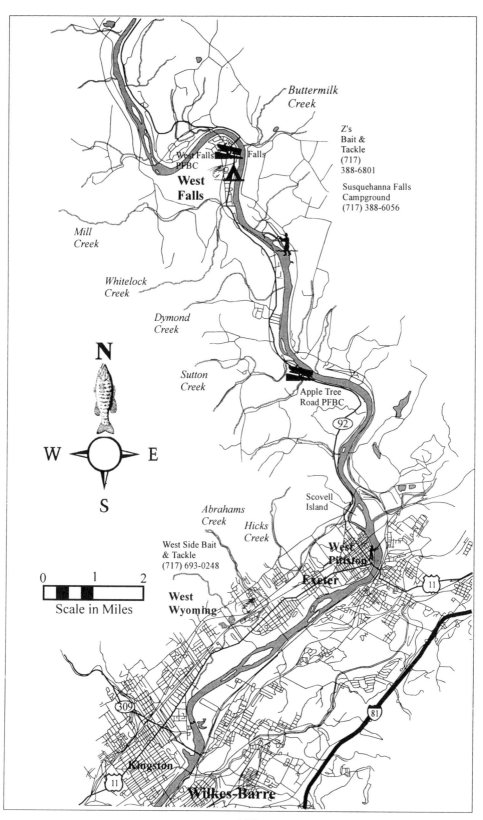

Buttermilk
Creek

Z's
Bait &
Tackle
(717)
388-6801

Susquehanna Falls
Campground
(717) 388-6056

West Falls Falls
PFBC

**West
Falls**

Mill
Creek

Whitelock
Creek

Dymond
Creek

N

Sutton
Creek

W ✦ **E**

S

Apple Tree
Road PFBC

92

Scovell
Island

Abrahams
Creek

Hicks
Creek

West Side Bait
& Tackle
(717) 693-0248

**West
Pittston**

Exeter

11

0   1   2

Scale in Miles

**West
Wyoming**

309

81

Kingston

11

Wilkes-Barre

Chapter 19

Lower West Branch Susquehanna

The lower West Branch of the Susquehanna has excellent fishing and canoeing opportunities. Despite coal mining in the middle reaches of the stream, the lower stretch has good populations of gamefish. The photographs on the walls of sporting goods stores in this area attest to good numbers of trophy-sized smallmouth, muskies, catfish, and even eels.

River access is reasonable and there are more campgrounds in this area than most. Many of them are privately owned and family oriented. Don't expect a wilderness experience, but at least you can take a shower, throw a round of horseshoes, and get an ice cream cone.

Another fun activity in this area is Reptiland. This small game park has dozens of interesting snakes, lizards, alligators and other animals in an attractive garden-like setting. An afternoon visit here is a fascinating and educational way to learn about a lot of creatures we won't bump into during our days on the river.

The upper end of this stretch of river brings us to the town of Williamsport. As you will see in the map and photograph, there is a small dam in Williamsport. The area immediately above the dam is dominated by power boats, water skiing, and similar activities so it's not the best for nature-oriented activities. Birders, fishermen, and canoeists will feel more at home below the dam. Fishing between the islands and in the tailrace area of the dam can be excellent.

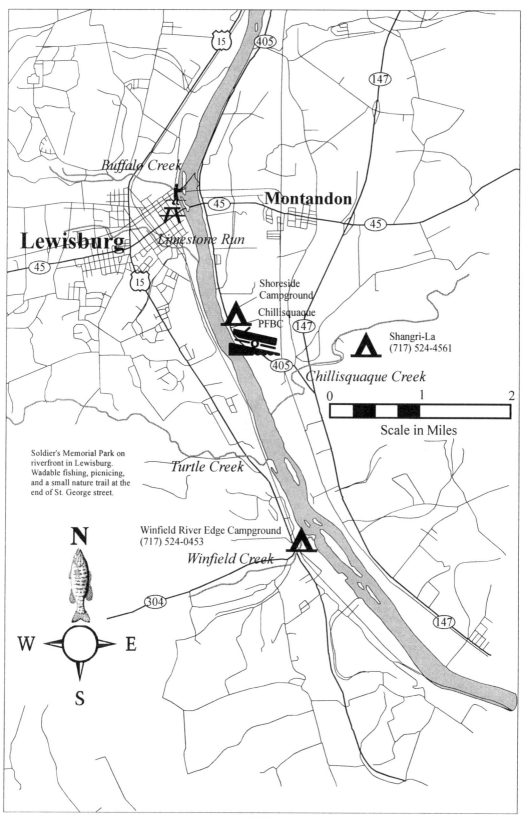

Buffalo Creek

Montandon

Lewisburg

Limestone Run

Shoreside
Campground

Chillisquaque
PFBC

Shangri-La
(717) 524-4561

Chillisquaque Creek

0   1   2

Scale in Miles

Soldier's Memorial Park on
riverfront in Lewisburg.
Wadable fishing, picnicing,
and a small nature trail at the
end of St. George street.

Turtle Creek

N

Winfield River Edge Campground
(717) 524-0453

Winfield Creek

W   E

S

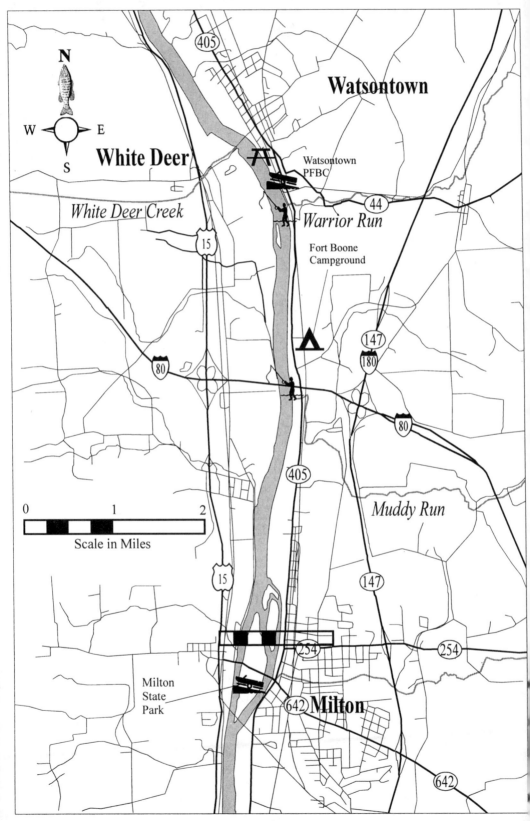

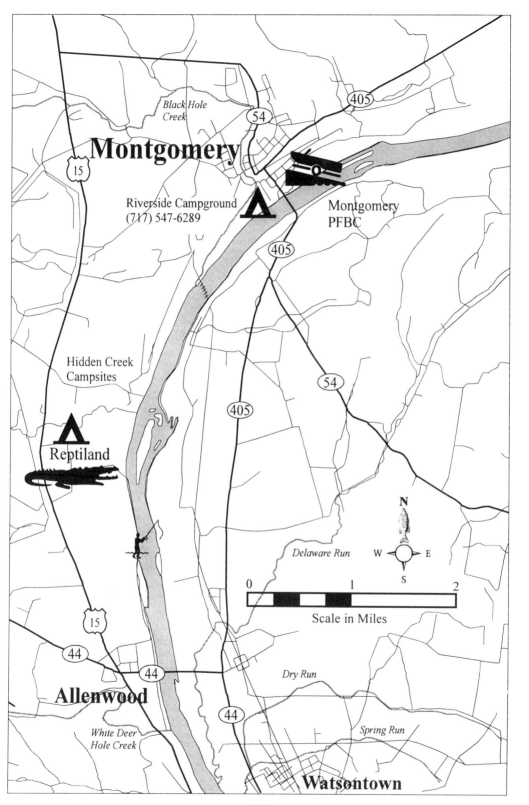

Black Hole
Creek

54

405

Montgomery

15

Riverside Campground
(717) 547-6289

Montgomery
PFBC

405

Hidden Creek
Campsites

405

54

Reptiland

N

Delaware Run

W   E

S

0   1   2

Scale in Miles

15

44

44

Allenwood

44

White Deer
Hole Creek

Dry Run

Spring Run

Watsontown

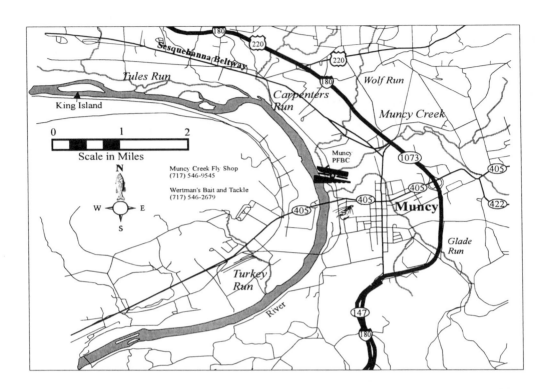

There are no alligators in the Susquehanna, but Reptiland is a fun place to see them!

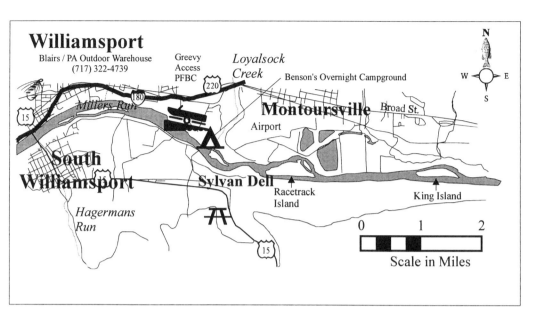

Williamsport

Blairs / PA Outdoor Warehouse
(717) 322-4739

Greevy
Access
PFBC

Loyalsock Creek

Benson's Overnight Campground

Montoursville

Broad St.

Airport

Millers Run

South Williamsport

Hagermans Run

Sylvan Dell

Racetrack Island

King Island

0   1   2

Scale in Miles

Williamsport dam and downtown

115

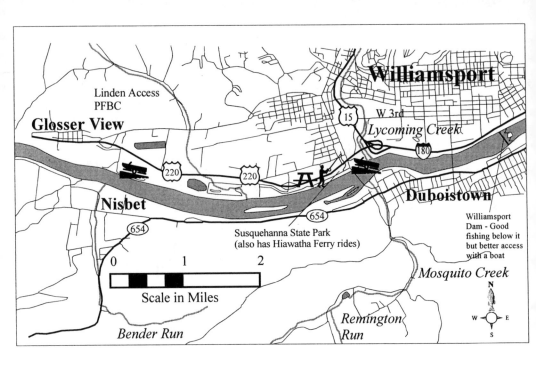

Williamsport

Linden Access
PFBC

Glosser View

W 3rd

Lycoming Creek

15

180

220

220

Nisbet

654

Duboistown

654

Susquehanna State Park
(also has Hiawatha Ferry rides)

Williamsport
Dam - Good
fishing below it
but better access
with a boat

Mosquito Creek

0   1   2

Scale in Miles

Remington
Run

Bender Run

N
W   E
S

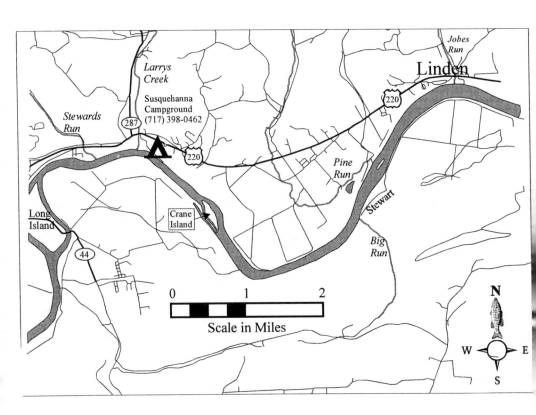

Jobes
Run

Larrys
Creek

Linden

Stewards
Run

Susquehanna
Campground
(717) 398-0462

287

220

220

Pine
Run

Long
Island

44

Crane
Island

Stewart

Big
Run

0   1   2

Scale in Miles

N
W   E
S

Index

R

Racetrack Island, 115
Redbuds Island, 85
Reed Island, 65
Reeds Island, 104
Reptiland, 110, 113
river stewardship, 41
Riverside, 104
Robert Island, 50, 53
Rockville Bridge, 90
Rookery Island, 68, 71
Rowland Island, 56

S

Safe Harbor Arboretum, 67
Safe Harbor Dam, 66, 69
Saginaw, 80
Sassafras Island, 84
Selinsgrove, 98
Shad Island, 71
Shady Nook, 98
Shamokin Dam, 101
Sheets Island, 86, 88
Shelley Island, 82
Shenk's Ferry, 66, 67
Shickshinny, 107
Shikellamy State Park, 100, 101
Shure's Landing, 53
Shures Landing Wildflower Area, 54
Sicily Island, 62
Silver Creek, 96
smallmouth bass, 7
Smallmouth Bass, 11
Smith's Falls, 51, 53
South Williamsport, 115

Spades Wharf Island, 84
spawning, 10, 18, 21
Spencer Island, 50, 53
spinning, 27
Steel Island, 50, 53
Steelton, 85
striped bass, 13, 47
Stucker Island, 85
Sunbury, 3, 6, 32, 99, 101, 103
sunfish, 16
Susquehanna flats, 47
Susquehanna River Trail, 94
Susquehanna Riverlands Park, 103, 107
Susquehanna State Park, 50, 53, 116
Susquehannock State Park, 31, 59, 60
Swatara Creek, 82
Sweigarts Island, 95
Sylvan Dell, 115

T

Tacquan Glen, 65
Three Mile Island, 79, 82
Toad Island, 96
Tri-County Club, 82
Turkey Point, 71
Turkey Run, 114
Turtle Creek, 111
Tydings Island, 48

U

Upper Bear Island, 62
Urey Islands, 65, 67
Urey Overlook, 67

W

Wade Island, 86
Wading, 4, 5, 38
walleye, 21, 76
Wapwallopen, 106
Warrior Run, 112
Washington Boro Islands, 71
water temperature, 5
Watsontown, 112, 113
Weise Island, 65, 67
West Branch of the Susquehanna, 110
West Fairview, 86
West Fall Island, 92
West Falls, 109
West Pittston, 109
White Deer, 112
Whites Island, 96
Wildcat Island, 62
wildflowers, 66
Wilkes-Barre, 108
Williamsport, 110, 115, 116
Winfield, 111
Wolf Island, 62
Wood Island, 50, 53
Wormleysburg, 86
Wrightsville, 73

Y

Yellow Breeches Creek, 85
York Furnace, 65
York Haven Dam, 76, 80, 82

Z

Zeigler Island, 95
Zimmerman Island, 84, 85

119

Map Key and Legend

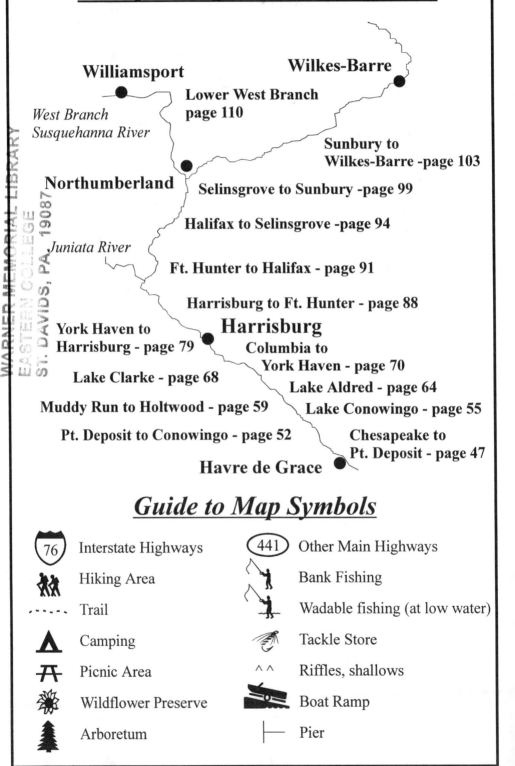

Williamsport

Wilkes-Barre

Lower West Branch
page 110

*West Branch
Susquehanna River*

Sunbury to
Wilkes-Barre -page 103

Selinsgrove to Sunbury -page 99

Northumberland

Halifax to Selinsgrove -page 94

Juniata River

Ft. Hunter to Halifax - page 91

Harrisburg to Ft. Hunter - page 88

York Haven to
Harrisburg - page 79

Harrisburg

Columbia to
York Haven - page 70

Lake Clarke - page 68

Lake Aldred - page 64

Muddy Run to Holtwood - page 59

Lake Conowingo - page 55

Pt. Deposit to Conowingo - page 52

Chesapeake to
Pt. Deposit - page 47

Havre de Grace

Guide to Map Symbols

76	Interstate Highways	441	Other Main Highways
🚶	Hiking Area	🎣	Bank Fishing
-----	Trail		Wadable fishing (at low water)
▲	Camping		Tackle Store
☷	Picnic Area	^ ^	Riffles, shallows
✿	Wildflower Preserve		Boat Ramp
🌲	Arboretum	⊢	Pier